CONCORDE

David Leney & Allan Burney

LONDON
IAN ALLAN LTD

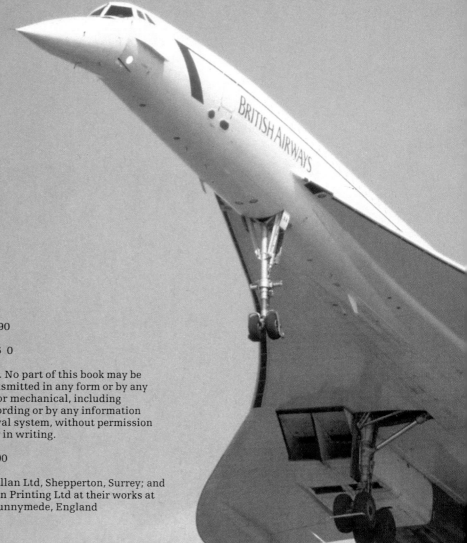

First published 1990

ISBN 0 7110 1896 0

Published by Ian Allan Ltd, Shepperton, Surrey; and
printed by Ian Allan Printing Ltd at their works at
Coombelands in Runnymede, England

Previous page:
Concorde head-on with visor and nose 'drooped'.

Right:
**Concorde adopts the familiar 'Praying Mantis'
pose as it approaches finals.** *K. Pettit*

Introduction

'Stand by — 3, 2, 1, now!'

Capt David Leney simultaneously presses the stop watch and bangs open the throttles which rapidly open up the engines to full power under their electric control.

As the speed builds and passes 60kt, the reheats cut in automatically, switches having been preselected before take-off. Viewed from the flightdecks of other aircraft waiting their turns to line up at the runway head behind Concorde, rosettes of flame flicker an instant and then blossom forth from the jet pipes of Concorde's four Olympus turbojets as she streaks down the runway.

In a haze of searing heat and swirling sulphurous exhaust gases the speed builds very quickly now as the Co-pilot calls '100kt'. 'Power set,' replies the Flight Engineer.

'V1 — rotate,' and the Captain eases back on the control column, rotating the aircraft to 15° pitch attitude.

The sleek white bird climbs swiftly away from Mother Earth in a shimmering shroud of heat. Speedbird Concorde 2 is airborne . . .

About the Author

The road to becoming a Concorde Captain had actually begun when David Leney had joined the Royal Air Force as a National Serviceman, training on Tiger Moths, Chipmunks, Oxfords and Vampires. These two years infected him with the flying bug and he turned down a university place to join a commercial pilot's course at Air Service Training, Hamble.

David was interviewed by BOAC and offered a job as a pilot, but first he had to complete the course for the Flight Navigator's Licence and navigate for one year before becoming a First Officer on one of BOAC's aircraft. He navigated Constellations and Argonauts until, in 1957, he began to fly as a Co-pilot of a Britannia. His career progressed as a Co-pilot or Navigator, converting on to the VC10 in 1963 and becoming a Captain in 1971.

In 1974 David joined the Pilot Management Team on VC10s, but in 1976 the chance came to 'bid' for Concorde. He was successful in his application and the six-month course was completed in June 1977, the first month in which he flew as a qualified Captain on the Concorde routes.

David retired as Captain in 1989 but still flies Concorde as co-pilot. He is married with four children and lives in Surrey.

Acknowledgements

Producing a 'From the Flightdeck' book is always a team effort and the author and photographer would like to thank the following for their valuable contribution to the project: all British Airways departments, especially Engineering TBB, friends in the Simulator Section and Public Relations. Special thanks go to the flight and cabin crews of 'Alpha Bravo's' New York-London flight and the round-the-world crew on 'Alpha Foxtrot'. The author is also grateful to Ken Pettit for photo-research, to Sharon Leney for her valiant effort in typing the manuscript and to Jonathan Falconer who has enthusiastically been involved with the project from start to finish.

Photographer's note

In a publication of this nature, it is quite impossible to photograph a representative Concorde flight in 'one shoot'. Therefore, we hope that readers will excuse the 'artistic licence' that is necessary to provide a set of illustrations that closely reflects the text.

All the photographs featured within this book were taken using a variety of Canon cameras and lenses. Allan Burney would like to thank Canon Cameras for their help in this project and in particular Jane Harvey, Canon Professional Services Controller.

NEW YORK . . .

The Captain of the British Airways Concorde from New York to London sits in his hotel bedroom and pondered over his career.

Twenty-five years ago he had sat in a hotel in New York as a Co-pilot on the BOAC Britannia service from New York to Boston and London. And then he had no idea that he would have been flying Concorde as a Captain for 12 years by the time 1989 arrived.

Below:
Concorde 'AB' taxies out at London Heathrow Airport on the first leg of her journey to New York John F. Kennedy Airport (JFK) on the evening before the author's crew will fly her back home. She will arrive at JFK at 5.50pm.

He goes downstairs to join his crew — the Co-pilot and Flight Engineer who are staying in the same hotel and the cabin crew, having driven in the crew bus from their hotel, were waiting outside.

They are all driven through the heavy traffic out of Manhattan through the Midtown Tunnel and on to Long Island. It is 07.45 and the journey can take anything from half-an-hour to an hour-and-a-half, depending on the traffic.

There is general talk in the bus about the 24hr spent in Manhattan and it seems the cabin crew had split up — three doing shopping and three going to the cinema. The three flightdeck crew had met for a meal late

on the previous afternoon and then had gone to bed fairly early remembering that 20.00 in New York was 01.00 the next morning in London.

They arrive at John F. Kennedy (JFK) Airport at 08.15 and make their way through the recently refurbished British Airways Terminal — the cabin crew to their waiting room and the technical crew to the Briefing/Operations Room downstairs.

The Captain had given the Co-pilot the westbound sector from London Heathrow (LHR) to JFK: this meant that the Co-pilot flew Concorde and the Captain acted as Co-pilot. It is general practice on the fleet to fly one sector each, so the Captain will handle the aircraft on this flight from JFK to Heathrow.

The crew are greeted like long-lost friends by the Operations Officer because he, like many crew members, has been part of the Concorde operation into and out of JFK since November 1977. There are two services a day from LHR to JFK and back, so crews spend many hours in New York and get to know operations staff very well.

Left:
New York — 7.20am: Capt David Leney, the author, leaves the hotel in Manhattan.

Below:
Rhapsody in gold: the morning sun begins to climb over the Manhattan skyline.

This page:
With the dew still thick on the grass beside the taxiway, Concorde 'AB' is towed to Gate 4 at JFK in the early morning, long before the crew and passengers are due to arrive.

Left:
In the Briefing/Operations Room the flightcrew make initial checks on fuel, flight plan and weather.

It is now time to get down to the paperwork which had been prepared very early that morning.

First the weather. A long computer printout of the weather for many airfields is studied. Of greatest interest is Heathrow where it is partly cloudy with a wind from the southwest at 20mph and the temperature at 13.00 Greenwich Mean Time (GMT) is 15°C. So no problems with London weather. What about JFK for the take-off? This can pose a problem well known to Concorde crews. The wind is from the northeast at 15mph, the sky partly cloudy and the temperature 10°C. This means that the

Left:
Proof of the weather at JFK: cloudy with occasional rain, despite the glorious sunrise.

use 4L for take-off. There are no restrictions on runway usage for landing.

The Port of New York Authority and the New York Air Traffic Controllers are extremely helpful on these occasions, and even though it causes them extra work, they always manage to fit Concorde into their traffic pattern with minimal delays.

However, it does mean that the aircraft will take extra fuel to cater for a possible take-off delay caused by using a non-conforming runway.

So the weather at each end of the flight is good — how about the en route airfields to be used in case some technical problem makes an en route landing necessary?

The chosen airfields are Bangor, Halifax, Gander, Santa Maria in the Azores, and Shannon. Concorde in its 12 years of Atlantic operations has visited all these airports, so it is known that each can provide the necessary facilities to cope with an unscheduled landing since they are international airports handling big jets every day.

Not only is the surface weather studied but charts are available giving the position of pertinent weather — cold fronts, depressions, warm fronts, thunderstorms and areas of high wind-jet streams. Although Concorde flies above almost all cloud, it still has to climb and descend through any weather at each end of the trip.

The weather situation seems routine so the Captain then turns his attention to the Fuel Flight Plan.

This is pre-prepared for him by the Operations Officer and the Co-pilot has been checking that the calculations are correct before the Captain looks at it and signs it. The flight plan is pre-computed for the JFK-LHR sector and then the corrections for the conditions of the day are added. There are three corrections:

● wind direction and speed for subsonic (below the speed of sound) flight
● wind direction and speed for supersonic flight
● a correction to cater for the air temperature deviations from the Standard Atmosphere.

These corrections are made by either adding or subtracting a fuel figure and a number of minutes. The fuel figure for the trip is adjusted and the final figure shows many kilogrammes are required. This figure is usually in the vicinity of 82,000kg and the time is usually

northeasterly Runway 4L will be in use and Concorde is not allowed to use this runway because it would fly over a very noise-sensitive area immediately after take-off.

In 1977 there were many people who did not want Concorde to operate from JFK, highlighted by a long, complicated legal battle and many demonstrations. Finally, it was agreed that Concorde could fly in and out of JFK if special procedures were observed and there were restrictions on the runways which could be used. These restrictions applied to all Concorde operations by both British Airways and Air France, which operates one Concorde per day from Paris to New York and back.

The weather conditions this morning mean that BA 002, the British Airways Concorde to Heathrow, will have to use the northwest-facing Runway 31L while other aircraft will

around 3hr 20min. Today it is 81,000kg and 3hr 17min.

The Captain then puts on any extra fuel he considers necessary. Today is Saturday and it is likely to be pretty busy at Heathrow so he decides to carry an extra 3,000kg for a possible short delay to his landing at Heathrow and 2,000kg for a possible take-off delay for reasons already explained (1,400kg is the normal taxying fuel). So the engineers will pump a total of 86,000kg on to Concorde today.

Another restriction on the fuel he can take is Concorde's Noise Abatement Take-off Weight. This is the maximum all-up weight for the aircraft so that when it takes off the noise measured by ground monitors will not exceed 112 decibels. The heavier the aircraft, the more power is required and, therefore, the more noise is made during the special Concorde Noise Abatement Procedure worked out before every take-off, not only at JFK but all airports from which Concorde operates.

The procedure (to be described in detail later) is basically one which requires the engine power to be reduced as the aircraft passes over any noise-sensitive area immediately after take-off. At JFK there are noise monitoring posts dotted strategically around the airport which record the number of decibels made by every departing aircraft and if 112 decibels is exceeded, the guilty airline is fined and the exceedence is recorded for statistical purposes.

Due to the quite complicated procedures carried out by Concorde crews the aircraft only occasionally violates the noise regulations, and quite often these violations are not the fault of crews or procedures. Different weather conditions alter the way noise reaches the ground. Other quieter aircraft also notch up violations from time to time.

The final thing to check before making their way to the aircraft is the state of navigation aids on the route, and approach and landing aids at each airfield which may be used. Another computer print-out is examined in detail which gives the most up-to-date infor-

Below left:
Meanwhile, passengers check-in at the Terminal Desk and make their way to the Concorde Lounge . . .

Below:
. . . where they are treated like VIPs by the attentive Passenger Handling Staff.

mation available to British Airways, enabling the crew to determine which procedure they will or will not be able to use at the destination. The serviceablity state of landing aids tells the Captain what minimum weather conditions he needs in order to begin an approach. Today, as the weather at Heathrow is good, no special landing aids are required but they are all expected to work normally.

The Load Control Officer completing the Concorde 'loadsheet' tells the Captain that on this flight there are 84 passengers, which is a good load, and ensures the service will operate profitably today. (A full load for Concorde is 100 passengers.)

The loadsheet is the legal document prepared for the Captain, showing him the number of passengers, the weight of passengers and baggage, the weight of fuel, the distribution of the load on the aircraft and the position of the centre of gravity — a particularly important aspect of loading on Concorde. The Captain has to sign this document making sure that every figure is correct and the whole aircraft is loaded in accordance with all the regulations laid down by law. The crew bid the operations staff farewell and walk to the aircraft.

Security restrictions stipulate that crews have to go through the same procedure as passengers prior to boarding the aircraft, so the crew baggage is passed through the X-ray machine. As they walk through the passenger lounge the crew bid 'Good Morning' to their passengers who have arrived early and who are taking advantage of the excellent facilities offered to Concorde passengers in the departure lounge.

This lounge is situated so that the passengers can see Concorde parked outside facing them and it is at this point that they get their first view of the white-painted fuselage and beautifully shaped wings. The crew also get their first glimpse of the Concorde they are going to fly to London — and they, too, never fail to appreciate the beauty of the Concorde shape.

The cabin crew have been aboard for about 15min now, preparing to receive the passengers and checking that the food on board is correctly stored and agrees with the comprehensive menu the passengers are given.

A Concorde cabin crew consists of a Cabin Service Director who is the senior cabin crew member. Under him/her are two pursers, one in each of the cabins and four stewards/stewardesses. There can be any combination of the sexes and they operate three to a cabin. They work extremely hard to give a very high

Above:
Outside on the ramp amongst the raindrops and puddles, baggage is loaded into the rear fuselage and forward underfloor holds of 'AB', which between them offer a total volume of 697cu ft.

standard of service in the short time available during the 3hr 20min flight.

The Captain and the Co-pilot immediately go to their seats on the flightdeck to begin their checks while the Flight Engineer completes the short safety check on the flightdeck. This

Above left:
Fuel uplift today will be 86,000kg of JET-A1, with some 2,000kg alone being used for taxying. A good impression can be gained here of the delta wing-shape, with the drooping elevons at the trailing edge.

Far left:
Concorde, in common with all other aircraft visiting JFK, is fuelled by means of a dispensing vehicle which draws fuel from an underground supply pumped from the remotely-sited fuel farm, via a hydrant connection, which can be seen in the left foreground of this picture.

Left:
Concorde's twin four-wheel main undercarriage bogies are equipped with lightweight carbon brakes, the first civil airliner to be so fitted.

Above:
This is the first glimpse of the compact flightdeck for the Pilot and Flight Engineer as they enter to begin their checks. In the immediate foreground on the right can be seen the Engineer's panel.

Above right:
Scene from the lounge: passengers' view of their aircraft as it is being fuelled.

ensures that there will be no danger to aircraft or personnel when the various systems are powered. He then goes outside to begin his external check during which he will check over 100 items, making sure that the ground engineers have not missed any part of the outside check. This is no reflection on the ground engineers' work, it is just another way of checking that the aircraft has been properly prepared by all concerned. During the check the fuelling process is still going on and will be completed only just before the passengers embark.

The check the Pilots are carrying out now is called a scan check: each Pilot — and later the Flight Engineer — sits in his seat and performs a check of all switches and instruments, oxygen systems and radios on his side of the aircraft. The whole process takes approximately 40min during which time the Flight Engineer has completed his outside check and has joined the two Pilots on the flightdeck to perform his scan check. At the end of the check the complete flightdeck is ready for the flight and the Captain will be able to call for the 'Before Start Check'.

During the scan check the Captain has loaded the three Inertial Navigation Systems (INS). Each set operates completely indepen-

dently, but a more accurate position can be obtained by mixing all positions. It is assumed that with three systems only two are indicating the correct position and if the third is out in any way it is discarded. Hence, an extremely accurate position can be obtained. The inertial system consists of accelerometers, placed on a gyro-stabilised platform, which measures acceleration in all directions, including the vertical, and computes this information to give navigation data, position, speed, track, heading and drift caused by wind. The Captain inputs the latitude and longitude of his present position (Gate 1 JFK) to the nearest 1/10th of a minute so that the INS knows exactly where it is. It is now able to give the present position of the aircraft at any time. A series of 'way-points' or positions over which the aircraft must fly are inserted into the computer, no more than nine at a time, and the aircraft can be flown, either manually or on auto-pilot from way-point to way-point. This will become more apparent later.

The Co-pilot is ready to distribute and use the paperwork he has collected from the operations planner. He gives the Captain a

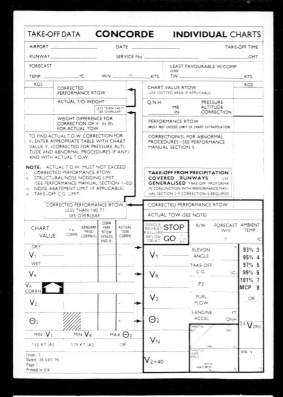

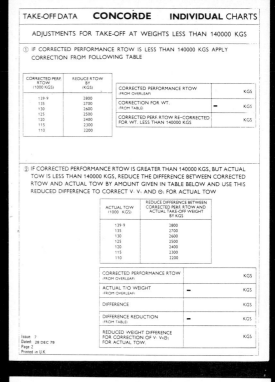

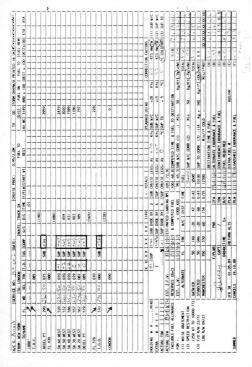

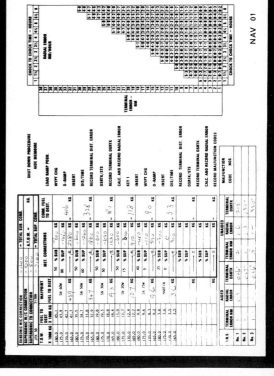

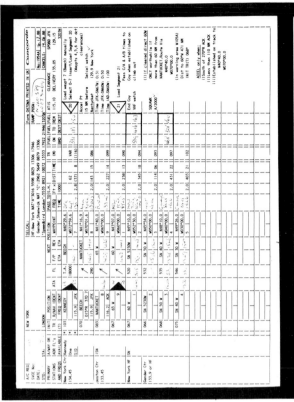

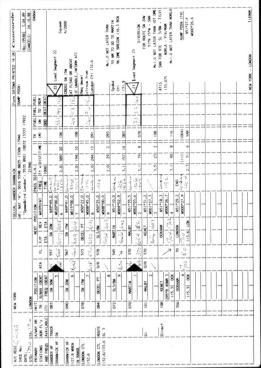

The paperwork needed for a flight — take-off proforma (above left); flight plan (below, far left); fuel plan (below left); communications plan (above).

copy of the Fuel Flight Plan, the Tactical Chart and the Communications Log. (He has previously checked all the books, manuals and documents which are required to be carried on each flight on a certain route.) He then starts the take-off calculation. First he needs the present weather conditions at JFK so he tunes into the Automatic Terminal Information Service (ATIS):

JFK ATIS 'This is Kennedy Airport information "K" at 12.50hrs. Two thousand scattered, 15,000 broken (*that was the cloud coverage*) visibility 10 miles, temperature 50 (°F), wind 010° at 10 (*wind direction and speed in kts*).'

This is all the weather information the Co-pilot needs to fill in the top part of the take-off form. He knows the projected take-off weight (fuel and the zero fuel weight of the aircraft) so he can, from the Performance manual, extract take-off speeds — known as 'V' for velocity — V1, VR, V2.

V1 is the go or no-go speed — ie, in the event of an emergency before V1 there is sufficient runway left to stop the aircraft, but if something happens after V1 the aircraft is committed to take-off.

VR is the speed to rotate, or the speed at which the Pilot begins to pull back on the control column to become airborne.

V2 is the safe climb-out speed in the event of an engine failure at the worst time — ie, soon after V1.

The relevant table for Runway 31L, the take-off runway, gives one more piece of information — Theta 2, or the attitude to which the pilot must rotate the aircraft during initial climb out.

The Co-pilot and the Flight Engineer separately working out the Fuel Flow and P7 (engine pressure) settings which must be achieved before take-off checks can be continued and the Co-pilot finally extracts from a table the Noise Abatement Time, engine power setting and throttle lever angle. It is so important on Concorde to get the engine power back at exactly the right time that it is easier for the Flight Engineer to pull the throttle back to a set position on the throttle quadrant (throttle lever angle) and then adjust engine power on the instruments forward of the throttles. The Co-pilot and Flight Engineer then compare their calculation to make sure they agree.

Concorde has now been refuelled and the Refuelling Engineer brings the Fuel Log and Technical Log to the flightdeck for checking and signatures. The Flight Engineer carefully checks that the fuel in the log agrees with the fuel that should be on board and hands the log to the Captain for this signature.

The Flight Engineer hands the Technical Log to the Captain who signs it, having checked fuel, oil and hydraulic oil uplift and any unserviceabilities there may be on the aircraft. He and the Engineer make sure that these 'snags' are acceptable for a return to base — London's Heathrow Airport — where they will be rectified. There is a comprehensive list of items which can or cannot be serviceable before take-off.

There is about 10min to departure now and the Co-pilot calls Air Traffic Control (ATC) for ATC Clearance. This is given by JFK 'Clearance Delivery' on VHF frequency 135.05MHz.

Co-pilot: 'Kennedy Clearance, this is Speedbird Concorde 002 with information "K" – IFR to London Heathrow (*IFR – Instrument Flight Rules*).'

Kennedy Clearance: 'Good morning Speedbird Concorde 002, you are cleared to London Heathrow, Kennedy One, Canarsie climb, Beech, direct Nantucket, then as filed. Maintain 5,000 and expect flight level 29.0 ten minutes after take-off, Squawk 1426.'

Left:
'Good morning Speedbird Concorde 2, you are cleared to London Heathrow.'

Right:
The Flight Engineer switches on engine feed pumps prior to starting the engines.

This means that Concorde is cleared to fly a Kennedy One departure which means that immediately after take-off turn left to Canarsie VOR (radio beacon) and then fly on a radial of 176° out of Canarsie to Beech. Climb to 5,000ft and then expect to climb to 29,000ft, 10min after take-off.

The way the Ground Controller can follow aircraft on his radar screen is for the crew to select a certain number on their transponder which shows up on his screen – hence Squawk 1426. By 'squawking' that number the controller will see the aircraft callsign BA 002, the altitude and the ground speed. This is the way nearly all terminal controllers keep abreast of the large number of aircraft in their area.

At this point the Before Start Check List is read out by the Co-pilot with answers from the Captain and the Flight Engineer, cross-checking altimeter settings and take-off speeds amongst many other items. One of the most important checks is the INS. The Captain reads out the 'Present Position' from the aerodrome folder (JFK is 40° 38.9' North, 73° 46.9' West) and each crew member notes this on the 'Communications Log'. It cannot be emphasised enough that it is vitally important that this position is correctly inserted into each INS. The Captain then reads the first three way-points that have been programmed into each INS, in this case Beech, Nantucket and 41° 40.0N, 65° 00.0W, and each crew member cross-checks his INS. When this check is complete the Flight Engineer switches each INS to 'NAV' on his panel and this automatically 'mixes' the three to give the most accurate navigation. Immediately after take-off one of the INS will be updated by JFK DME (Distance Measuring Equipment). This is an instrument showing the exact distance to ¹/₁₀th of one mile of the aircraft from the JFK

DME at any time. As the position of JFK DME is known, the INS automatically compares its calculated distance from JFK DME and updates itself. The overall accuracy can be shown by the fact that after the total distance from JFK to LHR has been completed, the INS positions are often less than one mile in error – that is one mile or less in 3,630 statute miles.

It takes a long time to narrate even half of the things that go on in and around Concorde before Speedbird 002 is ready to start. The time is 09.26 New York time (13.26 GMT) and the Flight Engineer calls the Ground Engineer who is standing underneath the nose of the aircraft by the nosewheel where he has an unobstructed view of the area under and around the aircraft.

Flight Engineer: 'Flightdeck to ground: are we clear to start engines?'
Ground Engineer: 'Ground to flightdeck clear to start. Ready to pressurise the right side.'

This means that the start truck supplying air to the turbines of the engines on the right side of the aircraft – air that turns the turbine when the Flight Engineer presses the start switch – is ready to be pressurised.

Flight Engineer: 'Pressurise the right-hand side.'
Ground Engineer: 'You have pressure on the right.'

The Flight Engineer can confirm this by looking up at the pressure in the duct indicated on his panel.

Flight Engineer: 'Starting three.'
Ground Engineer: 'Clear three.'

The Flight Engineer presses the No 3 engine start switch and when the high pressure side of the compressor (N2) reaches 10% he switches on the fuel at the high pressure (HP) cock. The engine slowly builds up to around 60% N2 which is normal idle speed and settles down. The Exhaust Gas Temperature (EGT) is around 240°C, at this stage No 2 engine is started and when both 3 and 2 are running the air start truck is disconnected.

From the inside of the aircraft there is a dull roar – from the outside there exists a very loud scream and people close to Concorde have to wear ear muffs or plugs. When the engines are running, electrical power is transferred from ground to aircraft power and the four generators are now on-line. Concorde is on her own and ready to be pushed back.

Above left:
'Chocks and ground equipment away. Signals from the left-hand side, thank you.' Concorde is pushed back with Nos 2 and 3 engines running and visor only down.

Left:
Once clear of the Terminal building, Nos 1 and 4 engines are started and Speedbird Concorde 2 is ready to taxi.

Above:
The Captain and Co-pilot (with checklist) complete the After Start Check List.

During the engine-start procedure the Captain is carrying out a complicated check of all his control surface movements. Concorde has three flying control systems; one mechanically-signalled hydraulically-powered system, and two electrically-signalled hydraulically-powered systems. The 'blue' electrical system is used normally and the 'green' is a standby. Electrical signalling means that when the control column is moved an electrical signal goes to the Power Flying Control Unit (PFCU) which hydraulically moves the elevon or rudder. The elevons are divided into three sections – inner, outer and middle, and the rudder into top and bottom to allow for failures of one section.

When Nos 2 and 3 engines are running the aircraft is ready to push back from the pier: a tractor pushes her back and away from the Terminal Building in order to start the other two engines. Nos 1 and 4 engines are then started from air bled from Nos 2 and 3 respectively.

The after-start checks are complete and the Co-pilot releases the ground engineer by calling:

Co-pilot: 'Chocks and ground equipment away. Signals from the left-hand side. Thank you.'
Ground Engineer: All equipment clear. Standby for signals from the left. Goodbye and have a good trip.'

He disconnects his headset and walks to the left out in front of the aircraft showing the Captain the nosewheel steering-pin and giving the 'thumbs-up' to indicate the aircraft is clear to taxi, as far as he is concerned.

| START UP Refer B1 | KENNEDY Clearance 135.05 348.6 | Ground 121.9 348.6 121.65 | Tower 119.1 258.3 | NEW YORK Departure 135.9 269.0 | ATIS 115.1 | D1 | L1 |

16 OCT 89

KJFK

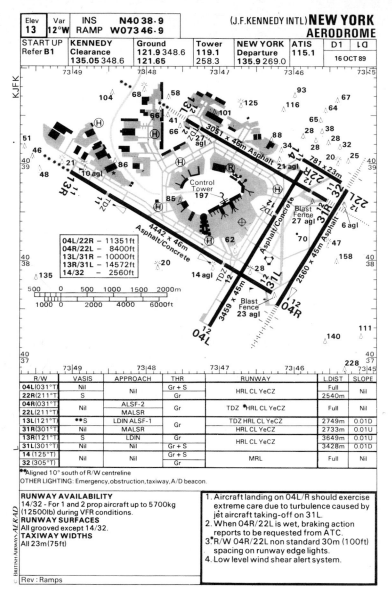

04L/22R – 11351ft
04R/22L – 8400ft
13L/31R – 10000ft
13R/31L – 14572ft
14/32 – 2560ft

4442 × 46m Asphalt/Concrete
3051 × 46m Asphalt
3459 × 45m
2560 × 45m Asphalt

Control Tower 197

Blast Fence 27 agl
Blast Fence 23 agl

Left:
JFK Aerodrome Taxi Chart.
Courtesy British Airways AERAD

Above right:
'Speedbird Concorde 2, clear to taxi right on the inner, left at Golf, right Zulu for Runway 31L.'

Right:
The distance between the pilots and the nosewheel makes taxying around corners more difficult.

R/W	VASIS	APPROACH	THR	RUNWAY	L.DIST	SLOPE
04L(031°T)	Nil	Nil	Gr + S	HRL CL YeCZ	Full	Nil
22R(211°T)	S		Gr		2540m	
04R(031°T)	Nil	ALSF-2	Gr	TDZ *HRL CL YeCZ	Full	Nil
22L(211°T)		MALSR				
13L(121°T)	**S	LDIN ALSF-1	Gr	TDZ HRL CL YeCZ	2749m	0.01D
31R(301°T)	Nil	MALSR		HRL CL YeCZ	2733m	0.01U
13R(121°T)	S	LDIN	Gr	HRL CL YeCZ	3649m	0.01U
31L(301°T)	Nil	Nil	Gr + S		3428m	0.01D
14 (125°T)	Nil	Nil	Gr + S	MRL	Full	Nil
32 (305°T)			Gr			

**Aligned 10° south of R/W centreline
OTHER LIGHTING: Emergency, obstruction, taxiway, A/D beacon.

RUNWAY AVAILABILITY
14/32 - For 1 and 2 prop aircraft up to 5700kg (12500lb) during VFR conditions.
RUNWAY SURFACES
All grooved except 14/32.
TAXIWAY WIDTHS
All 23m(75ft)

1. Aircraft landing on 04L/R should exercise extreme care due to turbulence caused by jet aircraft taking-off on 31L.
2. When 04R/22L is wet, braking action reports to be requested from ATC.
3. R/W 04R/22L non standard 30m (100ft) spacing on runway edge lights.
4. Low level wind shear alert system.

Rev : Ramps

© BRITISH AIRWAYS AERAD

Co-pilot: 'Kennedy Ground, Speedbird Concorde 002 is ready to taxi.'

Kennedy Ground Control, situated in the Control Tower replies:

'Speedbird Concorde 002 clear to taxi right on the inner, left at Golf, right Zulu for Runway 31L.'

The Co-pilot repeats the taxi clearance word for word to avoid any misunderstanding.

In the aircraft the Co-pilot selects the visor down and nose to 5°. Concorde pilots actually sit some 13ft back from the tip of the nose and if the nose is left in the up position it is difficult to see forwards and down when taxying, so the visor – which is the streamlining glass section – is lowered into the nose and the nose is dropped to 5°. The pilots now get a very good view of the taxiway ahead.

Taxying Concorde is quite difficult because the nosewheel is a long way ahead of the mainwheels and the Pilots are 38ft in front of the nosewheel. In a right angle turn the Pilots sit over the grass at the edge of the runway while the mainwheels are still on the centreline. It is similar in a way to driving an

Below:

With 5° of nose droop selected, Concorde approaches the runway holding point.

articulated lorry. It is fortunate the wingspan is only 84ft!

JFK Ground: 'Speedbird Concorde 2 – give way to the TWA 1011 at Delta and follow him.'

The Controller in the Tower has a magnificent view of the airport, and he needs this: in the busy periods in the late afternoon and early evening he controls up to 40 aircraft which are all taxying from or to the runways. He also has a very accurate ground radar if visibility is poor. Sometimes conversation is nonstop and it is difficult to get a word in on the ground frequency of 121.9MHz. It is something of a relief to the Pilots when the Ground Controller calls:

JFK Ground: 'Speedbird Concorde 2 – over to Tower 119.1. Have a nice day.'

The Co-pilot changes frequency and calls the Tower:

Co-pilot: 'Kennedy Tower, Speedbird Concorde 2 is with you approaching the holding point Runway 31L.'

JFK Tower: 'Speedbird 2, good morning. Hold short of Runway 31L – short delay.'

The delay is usually because all other aircraft are taking off on Runway 4L and Concorde has to wait to be fitted into the departure pattern.

The three flight crew have completed the Taxi Check which includes checking the flight instruments, engine controls and the transfer of fuel from tank No 9 in the forward fuselage to No 11 at the rear of the aircraft. Today there is 2,060kg to transfer in order that the centre of gravity (C of G) is exactly 53.5%. This transfer is calculated on the trim sheet or by computer and should give the exact C of G for take-off. If there is any error in the figures the whole calculation must be rechecked until the fuel is in the correct position. Meanwhile, the passengers have been briefed about the safety procedures and lifejacket drills and everyone is sitting down ready for the take-off.

Now for the most exciting and intricate part of the Concorde operation:

JFK Tower: 'Speedbird Concorde 2 is cleared for take-off Runway 31L.'
Co-pilot: 'Speedbird 2 is cleared to take-off 31L.'

The Captain eases Concorde on to the runway as close to the end of it as possible to make use of every metre of concrete in case the aircraft is forced to abort the take-off in the event of a systems failure.

Below:
The Co-pilot changes frequency from JFK Ground to JFK Tower: 'Speedbird 2, good morning. Hold short of Runway 31L . . . short delay.' A view from the flightdeck looking down the runway, waiting for take-off clearance.

Below right:
'Standby . . . 3, 2, 1, now . . .'

Far right:
. . . the Captain bangs open the throttles and the aircraft begins to accelerate rapidly.

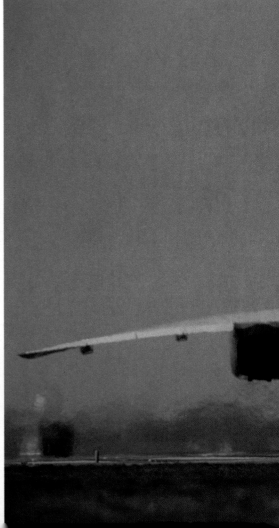

The Captain has called for the Before Take-off Check, on receipt of his take-off clearance, and the Flight Engineer is reading the short check list:

Flight Engineer: 'Take-off data and briefing update.'
Captain: 'No change to data or briefing. Cleared altitude 5,000ft set.'

After completing the rest of the check with the radar and transponder on, the Flight Engineer calls:

Flight Engineer: 'Before Take-off Check complete.'

Captain: 'Standby 3, 2, 1, now!'

He simultaneously presses the stop clock and bangs open the throttles which quickly open up to full power under their electric control. The aircraft begins to accelerate rapidly.

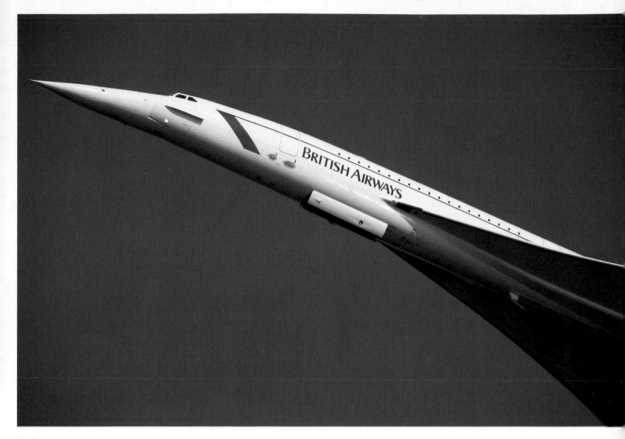

Left:
'Speedbird Concorde 2 airborne.'

Above:
The undercarriage is retracted and airspeed steadily increases as Concorde begins the subsonic climb.

Co-pilot: 'Speed building.'
The speed increases past 60kt — the reheats have cut in and the speed builds very quickly now.
Co-pilot: '100kt.'
Flight Engineer: 'Power set.'
He has four green 'go' lights in front of him.
Co-pilot: 'V1 — Rotate.'
The Captain positively pulls back on the control column and rotates the aircraft to 15° pitch attitude and Concorde climbs swiftly. Once the 15° has been reached and a positive rate of climb has been achieved, the Captain banks the aircraft using 25° bank angle to the left and Concorde — still only just above the water (300-500ft) turns away from the land and the noise-sensitive area. The precisely calculated noise time arrives:

Co-pilot: '3, 2, 1 — noise!'
The Flight Engineer simultaneously switches off the reheats and reduces power to the calculated setting for the aircraft weight and outside temperature. During the Noise Abatement Procedure 250kt is maintained and Concorde climbs more slowly. The pitch attitude to maintain 250kt with the reduced power is now in the order of 12°.

Co-pilot: 'Heading 235°.'
Captain asks for 'MCP' (*Maximum Climb Power*).

The aircraft is pitched up to maintain 250kt with full power and the bank angle is reduced to 7½° to increase the aircraft performance in order to make use of the fact that Concorde is now over the water and needs to climb as fast as possible before flying over the next piece of land which is a residential and beach area.

JFK Tower: 'Concorde 2 change to departure.'

Co-pilot: 'Concorde 2.'

This exchange is quick because all the crew are

Right:
During the Noise Abatement Procedure, 250kt is maintained and the aircraft banked left after take-off.

very busy at this time — no time for pleasantries.

Co-pilot: 'Departure, Speedbird Concorde 2 out of 2,000ft.'
JFK Departure: 'Controller, Roger Speedbird Concorde 2 climb to 5,000ft and turn on to a heading of 120°.'

On the 253° Radial from JFK VOR the aircraft must be above 2,500ft; Concorde is at 3,500ft and power is reduced: 'Bug Power.' The Flight Engineer sets the throttles back to the Noise Abatement power to cater for those people below and the aircraft climbs more slowly, but less noisily, away.

At 7nm DME from Canarsie VOR, climb power is restored, speed is increased and the fast climb to subsonic cruising altitude begins. Airspeed is steadily increased to VMO (maximum operating speed) and held there — 400kt. The rate of climb, of course, varies with weight but is in the region of 4,000ft/min.

Captain: 'Altimeter check.'

As 10,000ft shows in the altitude select meter, it gives the crew a warning when the aircraft is approaching 10,000ft. The Flight Engineer has started to move fuel back down the fuselage to tank No 11 to achieve a C of G of 55% during subsonic cruise.

Meanwhile the Co-pilot has been changing frequency rapidly from New York Departure on 135.9MHz to New York Centre to Boston Centre on 133.45 as the aircraft passes swiftly from the domain of one controller to his colleague next door, who takes control for a further segment of the climb. Both have already cleared Concorde to climb to Flight Level (F/L) 19.0 (on Standard Altimeter setting of 1,013.2mb — 2,992in) — ie, 19,000ft, and to fly direct to Nantucket which means that Concorde's INS is selected from its present position to 0-8 (way-point).

The Captain then engages the No 1 Autopilot and presses INS, Airspeed Hold (400kt) and makes sure 19,000 is in the Altitude Select (ALT SELECT) on the Automatic Flight Control System (AFCS) on the panel in the middle of the glareshield. He also sets both Automatic throttles to 'ON.' They remain in standby until the aircraft is acquiring 19,000ft, when they engage and maintain the present airspeed of

400kt. As the aircraft is approaching the desired altitude the Altitude Acquire (ALT ACQ) light illuminates and the Autopilot levels the aircraft off at this altitude. When level, the ALT HOLD light comes on. Concorde is now flying under Autopilot control at 19,000ft and 400kt towards Nantucket VOR (116.2MHz).

Boston Centre: 'Speedbird Concorde 2 is cleared to fly 29.0.'

The new altitude — 29,000ft — is set, the autothrottles disconnected and power is slowly increased. In order to maintain 400kt the Autopilot pitches the aircraft up and the final subsonic climb begins. The aircraft is still under the control of Boston until past Nantucket.

When level at 29,000ft the Captain talks to the passengers:

Captain: 'Ladies and gentlemen this is the Captain. We are now flying, as you can see on the panels on the front of each cabin, at 29,000ft and at a speed of 600mph over the water. Mach 1 is the speed of sound and we are at Mach 0.95 and will remain subsonic until we are over Nantucket Island. Those of you on the left-hand side of the aircraft can clearly see Martha's Vineyard and you will soon get a good view of Cape Cod. When we are over Nantucket Island we shall be cleared to climb and accelerate — climb to 50,000ft where we

achieve Mach 2, twice the speed of sound. This will equate to a speed of 1,350mph. To achieve the climb and acceleration I will apply full power and switch on the reheats or afterburners, two at a time. You will be able to see the speed building pretty quickly through Mach 1 up to Mach 1.7 when the reheats have finished their useful life on this flight and we switch them off again, two at a time. I will let you known when all this is happening.'

The climb check was completed at Mach 0.7 and now the Captain calls for the Transonic Check List. The Engineeer prepares the aircraft for supersonic flight and completes the check down to switching on the reheats. The INS is at its most accurate, having been updating on Hyannis DME and previously on JFK DME.

The moment that the passengers are waiting for — for those who have not flown on Concorde — is drawing close.

Co-pilot: 'Boston, Speedbird Concorde 2 request acceleration and climb clearance.'

Boston Centre: 'Speedbird Concorde 2 standby, I have traffic at FL330, opposite direction, expect climb in 20 miles.'

This is exactly right because Concorde is allowed to climb 15 miles before Nantucket

Below:
The sleek profile of Concorde is well shown in this view as the aircraft climbs-out after take-off.

Below:
New York
Courtesy Jeppesen Sanderson Inc

1 INCH = 40 NAUTICAL MILES

because the sonic boom does not reach the ground until after passing the island, and therefore falls in the water, upsetting only the occasional sailor.

The clearance soon comes;

Boston Centre: 'Speedbird Concorde 2 cleared to climb to the block 55.0 to 59.0 cross 67°W above FL43.0.'

The Captain understands this to mean that Concorde may climb to FL55.0 and then has a block of altitude from 55,000 to 59,000ft in which to operate.

Co-pilot: 'Speedbird Concorde 2 is cleared to the block 55.0 to 59.0 — Mach 2.'

Captain: 'Ladies and gentlemen — the Captain — we have been cleared to climb and increase speed so I am increasing power and switching on the reheats in 30 seconds.'

The Captain selects 59,000ft in the ALT SELECT, presses Pitch Hold on the AFCS and disconnects the autothrottles and pushes the throttles slowly forward to maximum climb power, simultaneously pitching Concorde up by 2°-3° to contain the speed below VMO and begin the climb.

Flight Engineer: 'Inboard reheats on, outboard reheats on.'

The Engineer switches on the reheats and carefully monitors all the engine parameters, especially the nozzles at the rear of the engine which become divergent as the extra power is applied. The aircraft begins to accelerate quickly towards Mach 1 and the transition to supersonic speed is so smooth that the only way passengers can tell is to watch the Flight Information panels in the front of each cabin. These give details of altitude, outside air

Below:
During the Transonic Check List the Flight Engineer resets the engine intake controls preparing the aircraft for supersonic flight.

Above:
During the transonic acceleration, the cabin crew begin the meal service to passengers.

temperature, distance to go in statute miles and — very important — the Mach number. It often seems a pity that this momentous transition through the speed of sound is so uneventful, but the Concorde designers obviously got it right.

On the flightdeck the passing of the shock wave along the aircraft is seen on the pressure instruments as the wave passes the static vents on the side of the forward fuselage. The rate of climb and descent indicator fluctuates and the main servo altimeters also fluctuate, but because the aircraft is in Pitch Hold nothing is felt except the acceleration when the reheats are switched on. The Captain tells the passengers it feels like two small 'pushes in the back', but it gives an increase of thrust in the region of 20% and eases Concorde through the high drag area between Mach 0.97 and 1.3 and is left on until Mach 1.7.

Part of the Flight Engineer's transonic check list is to begin the movement of the fuel back to tank No 11 once more. As the speed increases the centre of pressure (lift) moves aft, so the centre of gravity must be moved aft also to keep the aircraft in balance, and this is

achieved by pumping almost 6,000gal back from the front fuselage tanks into tank No 11 at the rear. The C of G moves from 55% to 59% during the acceleration.

An interesting phenomenon occurs in the flight envelope when 32,000ft is passed. Whereas before, the VMO (maximum operating speed) was 400kt at this weight, when the altitude passes 32,000ft the VMO increases and MAX CLIMB is selected on the AFCS so the speed is allowed to increase to follow the VMO pointer. The idea is for the speed to be exactly the same as VMO, thereby allowing the aircraft to operate at its most efficient speed — as fast as is structurally possible.

Maximum climb speed is maintained and the reheats are switched off at Mach 1.7 at approximately 43,000ft and the fuel flow meters adopt a more normal rate of fuel usage. When the reheats were used on take-off the fuel flow was in excess of 80,000kg/hr (for approximately one minute) and when they were selected at 29,000ft the flow was 44,000kg/hr for not more than 15min. Having switched off the reheats the aircraft obviously climbs and accelerates more slowly and this is governed by aircraft weight and, to a greater degree, by temperature. If the temperature is below International Standard Atmosphere — a hypothetical temperature used to relate outside air temperature to a standard figure — then the aircraft will climb and accelerate more rapidly. If the temperature is above ISA it may take a considerable time to achieve 50,000ft where Mach 2 is reached. If the temperature is low, Mach 2 is reached quickly and the aircraft is ready to begin the cruise climb.

Speeds greater than Mach 1 cannot be reached at all without the aid of the square intakes in the front of each engine. The design of these intakes is absolutely crucial to the whole operation of Concorde, and the test flying required to perfect this design was prolonged and often fraught with problems. What has emerged is an excellent and trouble-free system.

Air cannot be accepted smoothly into the engine at speeds much above Mach 1, so the airflow has to be compressed and slowed down to enter the engine below supersonic speed, even though the aircraft is flying at twice the speed of sound. This is achieved by using ramp doors which are opened into the intake causing shock waves to form in four places focused on the bottom edge of the intake. The air is slowed down from Mach 2 to Mach 0.5 and the engine runs smoothly. The intake doors are hydraulically-powered computer-controlled and therefore fully automatic, depending on the speed of the aircraft.

When the throttles are moved towards the closed position and less air is required by the engine, spill doors at the bottom of the intake open to allow excess air to escape. This also allows smooth running of the engine and the ramps modulate to improve the situation.

The Flight Engineer is continuously monitoring the intakes during the various phases of supersonic flight because if the ramp does not work properly and the automatic transfer of control does not move from one system to the other, a surge may occur. This means that too much air is trying to pass through the intake and the engine cannot accept it. The smooth flow is interrupted: a rumbling noise and vibration is felt, sometimes very loudly, and the air flow becomes rough. This usually happens very suddenly and immediate drills are required of the crew. The idea is to throttle back all engines until the surging engine is identified and the other three can be restored to cruise power. The surging usually stops when the engine is throttled back. The passengers and the cabin crew are surprised by the ensuing rumbling noise and the Captain quickly explains the reason over the PA. This surging occurred quite frequently when Concorde first began passenger service but the reliability of the intakes became much better and it is now a very rare occurrence.

Up until 67° West longitude, Concorde has been controlled by Boston Radar and communications have been on VHF but at 67°W things change:

Boston Centre: 'Speedbird Concorde 2, radar service is terminated. You are cleared to en route frequency. So long.'

The Co-pilot acknowledges and begins to take No 1 High Frequency (HF) set to 8825 kHz and calls New York.

Co-pilot: 'New York, this is Speedbird Concorde 2 on 8825.'

HF reception is usually quite good on the Atlantic (not as good as VHF) but controllers are very busy with aircraft in a very large section of the Atlantic approaching or flying past New York, but not in VHF range. After a while New York replies:

New York: 'Speedbird 2, this is New York Radio, go ahead.'
Co-pilot: 'New York Speedbird 2, past 67W at 14.22, Flight Level 440, estimating 60W at

14.42. The wind is 240/20 the temperature −52°, requesting Selcal check BDEG.'

Selcal is a useful system which can alert crews to a call from a station by a code, and when this code is activated by the station a light illuminates on the front console and a gong sounds. This allows pilots to take off their headset during HF communications and still maintain a watch on the frequency. New York reads back the message:

New York: 'Here is your Selcal.'
The light comes on and the gong sounds and the Co-pilot acknowledges:
Co-pilot: 'Selcal checks OK.'

He then, with relief, takes off his headset and relaxes for a while.

Concorde has two VHF sets and two HF sets and they are now set up as follows. Frequency 'A' on No 1 VHF is set to the International Emergency frequency of 121.5MHz and the loudspeaker in the flightdeck on the Captain's side is switched on. This means that the crew can hear messages transmitted on 121.5 in flightdeck without wearing their headsets. If they wished to transmit themselves they would have to don their headsets in order to use the microphone.

'B' frequency on No 1 VHF set is tuned to the next VHF frequency to be used when VHF communication is resumed – in this case Shanwick Ocean Control on 127.9MHz but it cannot be used until the changeover switch is moved from A to B. No 2 VHF 'A' frequency is selected to 131.8MHz, which allows aircraft to communicate with each other when crossing the Atlantic. Concorde can often help small aircraft which, because they are flying lower, do not remain within VHF range as long as very high flying aircraft, so messages can be relayed. The other No 2 frequency is set to 129.9 – 'Air Inc' – a service which allows airliners to transmit messages to their company in the USA via this frequency. This is a very useful service which companies are happy to pay for.

No 1 HF is set to 8825 – New York in this case – although Gander (Newfoundland) and Shanwick (Shannon/Prestwick) are also using the same frequency. No 2 HF is set to a frequency which will broadcast, at set times, the weather forecasts and actual weather at certain stations.

The first weather situation the crew wishes to know is Halifax in Nova Scotia so the Co-pilot tunes No 2 VHF to 121.0 which gives the Air Traffic Information Service (ATIS) at

Halifax continuously. It is usually updated every hour, or more frequently if bad weather is being experienced and things are changing. The runway and let-down procedure in use at Halifax are also given.

Crews need to know the weather at any time at an enroute diversionary airport where they can land if something prevents them carrying on to London – an engine problem for instance – and Concorde crews are provided with a Tactical Chart to be used on the Atlantic route. This chart shows at a glance where a pilot can divert if he has an engine problem and has to decelerate to subsonic speeds and fly at normal altitudes (35,000ft) on three engines. The double or two-engine failure case is also plotted. This chart is continually monitored because a decision has to be made quickly. Roughly halfway across the Atlantic the decision to go on to Shannon or back to Gander must be taken in the case of failures, or even divert to Santa Maria in the Azores which may have better weather than the other two airports.

Right:
The Co-pilot turns to speak to the Flight Engineer (note that the sun is beginning to set behind Concorde).

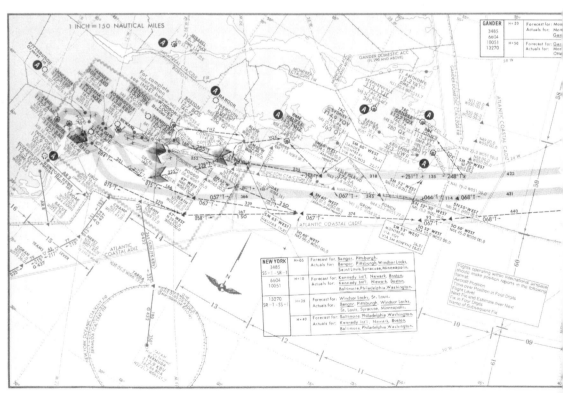

By the time the aircraft has reached 50,000ft (FL50.0) the Flight Engineer has moved the required fuel into tank No 11 at the rear and is now continually monitoring intakes, electrics, hydraulics and, of course, fuel. There are 13 tanks and the use of fuel in the correct order of tanks – both ensuring fuel to all engines and also maintaining the correct centre of gravity – is a job which requires continuous monitoring. The fuel may not always be consumed evenly across the aircraft so the Flight Engineer balances the fuel in each wing by transferring fuel across the aircraft. He always informs the pilots that he is changing fuel situations so that one other person is 'in the loop' while movement is taking place. When he is not fulfilling purely engineering duties he obtains the weather on HF.

Printed on the Jeppesen Concorde High Altitude Enroute Atlantic Chart are details of weather broadcasts: Gander, Halifax and Goose Bay amongst others broadcast at 20 and 50min past the hour; Shannon transmits Shannon, Prestwick, Heathrow, Manchester and Gatwick weather at 5 and 35min past the hour; and Paris and Santa Maria at 45min past the hour. The Engineer copies them on to a weather report form and hands them to the

pilots. The crew together can then decide on the best tactical plan should any adverse situation develop and they will have everything at their fingertips. This not only caters for emergencies but gives the Captain the information he requires for his next message to the passengers.

'Ladies and gentlemen, as you can see on the displays in the front of each cabin we have reached 50,000ft and Mach 2. Mach 2 is twice the speed of sound, 1,325mph, 22.5 miles/min or to put it one more way, one mile in 2.75sec – and that is Concorde. She still wants to go faster but we don't allow that. We maintain Mach 2 and, as the aircraft uses fuel and therefore her weight decreases, we allow her to climb to between 50 and 60,000ft. We expect to reach 58,000ft before we have to decelerate and descend. The Concorde route always takes us south of Halifax in Nova Scotia, south of Gander in Newfoundland across the Atlantic to pass south of Ireland and make our landfall at a place called Combe Martin in North Devon –

Below:
The Concorde High Altitude Enroute Atlantic Chart. *Courtesy Jeppesen Sanderson Inc*

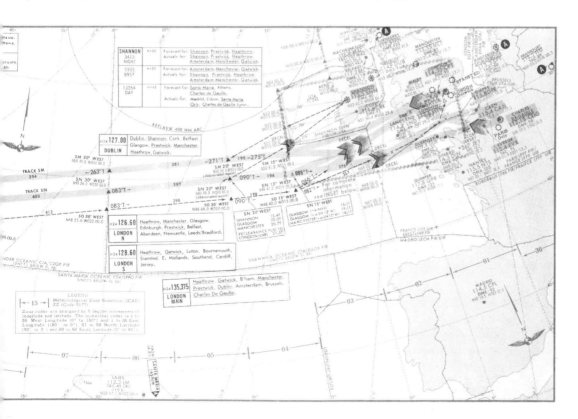

over the West Country. Toward's London's Heathrow Airport where the weather is fine — the temperature is 15°C, 59°F, and we shall be landing to the west necessitating passing to the south of Heathrow and over the West End of London. It is now 2.42pm in London, if you would like to set your waches — 2.42pm — and we shall arrive, on schedule, at 6.10pm. I will leave you in peace to enjoy your lunch and speak to you just before we start to slow down.'

Concorde is now flying in the MAX CRUISE mode of the autopilot. This means that the autopilot is restricted by the lowest of three parameters. It will maintain Mach 2 unless the maximum allowable indicated air speed (VMO) is exceeded or the maximum allowable Total Air Temperature (TMO) is exceeded when the automatic throttle which is selected — but is in standby mode — engages and reduces the speed to decrease whichever parameter is controlling. The autopilot may pitch the aircraft up to assist in speed reduction. As soon as a stable Mach number is achieved everything returns to normal. This sequence of events may not

Below:
The Cabin Service Director is responsible for the excellence of the service to his passengers.

occur on the sector if the outside air temperature is stable.

The temperature on the nose of the aircraft varies greatly from take-off to landing. During subsonic flight the temperature on the nose reflects, approximately, the actual outside air temperature. During subsonic cruise the outside air temperature is around −50°C however, as airspeed increases, the temperature on the nose skin increases as kinetic heating increases and, at Mach 2, can peak at 127°C (TMO). This is close to the maximum allowable for the aluminium alloys used in the majority of Concorde's structures. It is interesting to note that the whole aircraft expands 8-10in when it is at Mach 2 and hot, and then contracts when it cools down during deceleration.

A complete fuselage was built at Farnborough during the early days and was subjected to thousands of simulated cycles to see how the structure stood up to this extremely hostile environment. So far the actual aircraft have behaved themselves exactly as the test fuselage and shows how well the designers succeeded all those years ago. It is worth noting that the design was frozen in 1965.

In the cabin, the cabin crew — three in the front cabin, three in the rear — are serving passengers with lunch. Or is it lunch? Because the time in London is 3pm and in New York 10am, maybe 'Morning Meal' is the best description.

The Concorde menu is very comprehensive, and wines are carefully chosen. The menu is changed for each service once every two weeks so the businessmen who travel frequently do not have the same meal every time. Because of the size of the fuselage — very long and narrow — careful planning of tray content and serving routine takes place. A full First Class service is not possible for the above reason and also because time is very limited. The vast majority of passengers are extremely satisfied with the Concorde service and the cabin crew work very hard to achieve this in the 3hr 20min flight time.

Passengers are mainly businessmen or women and most work on the aircraft for their meetings on arrival or next morning. Many make connections through Heathrow to all parts of the world. The arrival time at London enables connections to be made with British Airways flights to Africa and the Far East and Australia as well as most destinations in the UK and Europe.

Celebrities often travel on Concorde to shorten the time of their journey before making appearances in London – often the same evening.

The three crew on the flightdeck are also enjoying their meal. They all eat together again as there is no time to stagger meals and each pilot must choose a different meal from his colleague for reasons of safety, minimising chances of incapacitation through food poisoning. Although this is a time for comparative relaxation, radio calls still have to be made during the meal.

Calls are made at 50°W, 40°W to Gander Radio; at 30° to Gander and Shanwick; and at 20°W and 15°W to Shanwick, before changing to VHF at 15°W. The word 'Shanwick' is a mixture of Shannon and Prestwick – the Oceanic Control is at Prestwick having moved from Shannon in Ireland, but the Controllers are Irish.

Co-pilot: 'Gander, copy Shanwick – Speedbird Concorde 2 is Sierra November 30° West at

Right:
Champagne service — corks pop as Concorde approaches the sound barrier.

Below:
As Concorde climbs towards cruise height, the sky above becomes noticeably darker.

Left:
While the passengers are enjoying the very best in food and wine, up at the sharp end the flightdeck crew are hard at work. In the left-hand seat the Captain is pictured with the Communications Log on his lap during the cruise at 57,000ft.

Below left:
Passengers in the cabin experience a truly excellent meal . . .

Below:
. . . as can be appreciated from the Concorde menu and wine list. *British Airways PLC*

NEW YORK · LONDON

L U N C H

A P P E T I Z E R S
Canapé selection including, lobster, galantine of smoked goose and fresh asparagus

Papilotte of smoked salmon and trout mousse Served with tiger prawn and a croustade of caviar pearls

M A I N   C O U R S E S

Tender grilled fillets of lamb, chicken and pork, flavoured with fresh herbs. Served with baby turnips, zucchini, tomato and almond potatoes

or

Goujons of Dover sole with bay scallops in saffron sauce accompanied by spinach, tomato and pilaf rice

NEW YORK · LONDON

15.50. Flight Level 55.0 (*50,000ft*), estimating Sierra November 20°W at 16.10. The wind is 250/40kt and the temperature −55°C, over.'

Gander: 'Speedbird Concorde 2 copy Shanwick.'

Shanwick then comes back with confirmation that he has copied the message. The Co-pilot asks Shanwick for a Selcal check which is received and Shanwick has now assumed radio control of the aircraft.

During the flight Concorde has so far spoken to two other aircraft. One was having difficulty raising Gander from 7,000ft — he was ferrying a light aircraft from Gander to Shannon on his way to Frankfurt finally, and the other was an executive jet who wanted to know what Corcorde's speed was as he passed below. He wondered if he would feel the shock wave as Concorde passed directly over him. No further comment was received.

At 60°W, 50°W, 30°W, 20°W and 15°W fuel checks are carried out. At the precise time of passing these points the Flight Engineer calls out the fuel on board. The Pilots both enter this figure on the Communications Log, subtract the calculated fuel to Heathrow and this gives them the fuel remaining at destination. In this case the figure is 14,800kg (14.8 tonnes). 9,200kg is required to divert to

---

Gatwick for any reason with 6,500kg remaining at Gatwick as reserve fuel. Therefore, 14,800−9,200=5,600kg for holding fuel — ie, fuel to allow for any Air Traffic Control delays (5,600kg is equivalent to approximately 25min holding time). This fuel situation is typical and Concorde very rarely diverts to an alternate due to a fuel situation. The usual reason is weather, but the total number of diversions is very few.

When the passengers have finished their meal, many of them like to visit the flightdeck. On a subsonic big jet, the Captain usually goes into the cabin to talk to passengers individually. This can take up to an hour and this time is not available to a Concorde Captain, nor is he able to visit the cabins during the meal service because he would only hinder the efficient flow of things, so he invites as many people as are interested to visit the 'sharp end'.

People are generally overawed by the number of instruments and the apparent complexity of the small flightdeck. One of the crew, often the Flight Engineer because he is the first person passengers meet on the flightdeck as they enter, explains a few points of interest to them. Nose and visor operation, expansion of the aircraft, speed and altitude are the favourite subjects. Crews have to explain that the flightdeck is very close to the extreme point of the aircraft and this is why it appears cramped. The Captain will point out the darker blue of the sky at altitudes of 55,000ft and above. Most passengers are puzzled that there is no sense of speed at all — the aircraft appears to be standing still in the air because the air is very smooth at the higher altitudes. If clear air turbulence has caused Concorde to give a bumpy ride, the crew have to explain that the probable cause was a

Below:
The Flight Engineer is copying details of weather broadcasts.

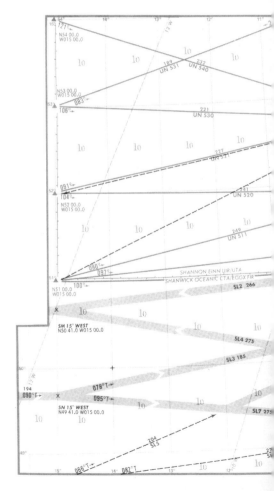

horizontal temperature variation or sheer, and this does cause bumpy conditions but thankfully only occurs occasionally.

Many photographs of the flightdeck are taken and these pictures are only outnumbered by those taken of passengers standing in front of the 'Mach 2.00' signs in the cabins.

At 20°W longitude the crew must begin preparing for the deceleration and descent. The sonic boom carpet is the main cause of deceleration restrictions and in order to prevent the shock wave reaching land as a sonic boom, Concorde must be subsonic at least 35 miles from any land behind or ahead, and less than 20 miles either side of the aircraft's path. Concorde therefore has to be at Mach 1 some 55nm from Combe Martin in North Devon — or MARTIN as it is called on the communications log.

There are two booms — or shock waves — which are felt near the aircraft's path. The first is called the Primary Boom which is two shock waves directly from the aircraft to the ground:

it can be compared to the bow wave from a boat and is easily controllable by decelerating Concorde so as to prevent the boom reaching land. This boom is loud and unacceptable for the people living under the aircraft's flightpath. It has been likened to the sound of heavy gunfire in the immediate vicinity of the listener.

The second, and much less noisy and disturbing boom, is felt by people a long way from the aircraft's flightpath. It is two shock waves which are, of course, primary to begin with, but go up into the atmosphere and are reflected down to earth again. The shock wave in its descent to earth is often diverted in its path by very strong winds at very high levels and by temperature variations in the atmos-

Below:
The western approaches to MARTIN and the transonic deceleration point.
Courtesy Jeppesen Sanderson Inc

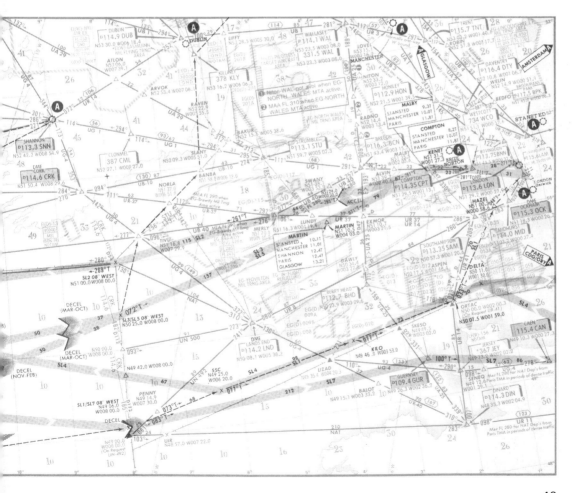

DESCENT AND LANDING DATA — *Concorde*   **British Airways**

				DH / QNH	DH / RA	RVR / VIS	DH / QNH	DH / RA	RVR / VIS
AIRFIELD		SAFETY ALT	FT						
LANDING WT		TRANS LEVEL	F/L						
V REF	-	RUNWAY							
INCREMENT		SEC SAFETY ALT	FT			FT			
VTT		START FINALS ALT	FT			FT			
		O.M. ALT	FT			FT			
FUEL AT DESTINATION		REG LDG WT	T			T			
	T	MINIMA	DH / QNH	DH / RA	RVR / VIS	DH / QNH	DH / RA	RVR / VIS	
DIVERSION FUEL TO:—									
		ILSH							
		ILSC							
		ILSC2							
	T	T	ILSC3						
HOLDING FUEL		RUNWAY ELEVATION	FT			FT			
	T	T	GO AROUND ALT	FT			FT		
BRIEFING TRIGGERS:—									
RED. NOISE APP. — VASIS — PAPI — GLIDE SLOPE — DISPLACED THRESHOLD									

LANDING WT	96	98	100	102	104	106	108	110	111	113	T
V REF	150	152	154	155	157	158	160	161	162	163	KNOTS

BA2140

Left:
The throttles are closed further during the deceleration.

Below left:
Concorde Descent and Landing Data card.
British Airways PLC

phere. It is felt as a distant rumble and often windows rattle as the wave hits them. No damage is ever caused by these booms. Concorde Captains vary their deceleration points from summer to winter to try and keep the Secondary Boom off the Southwest of England, and off Long Island on the other side of the ocean. In summer, Concorde is subsonic 55nm from Combe Martin, in winter the subsonic point is 105nm from the same point. It would be more simple, from an operational point of view, to alter the track of the aircraft approaching England and Wales, but the narrow area up the Bristol Channel precludes this option and Concorde, therefore, suffers a fuel penalty by decelerating early in the months between 1 November and 1 March. Going into New York the track is changed and Concorde can stay supersonic longer between May and August. The French Concorde comes up the English Channel and many secondary booms have been heard in the Channel Islands and on the south coast of England. There also, the option of changing the routeing of the aircraft is not available.

The Captain asks for the Deceleration and Descent Check List and the Flight Engineer asks the Pilot to check the following:

Warning and Landing Display. He checks the integrity of the Automatic Landing System by pressing a button which puts on all the warning lights which could illuminate due to failure of the autopilot — or failure of the pilot when he is flying Concorde manually — to remain within the limits of the ILS.

Safety Heights. The Pilots and Engineer together check the lowest heights available, due to high ground, to which the aircraft may descend during the approach into London Heathrow. The highest safety height is 3,500ft west of Reading, becoming 2,300ft close to the airport. Once the aircraft is under radar control from the ground, both the pilots and the Ground Controller will be conscious of the safety heights during the approach.

Altimeters. The Pilots set up the white 'bugs' on the outside ring of the altimeters — first the main Servo Altimeter used during the descent

to final approach. These bugs are set at 80ft which is the height of the airfield above sea level, and at 380ft which is the Decision Altitude below which the aircraft may not descend unless pilots have visual contact with the runway. The Radio Altimeter, used in the final stages of the approach, is set to 300ft and is purely advisory in this case because the pilot is going to fly a manual approach. If the weather is marginal or a practice automatic landing is to be carried out, the Radio Altimeter bug is set to various settings from 200 to 15ft, depending on the decision height during the automatic approach. When the aircraft approaches the Radio Altimeter decision height a warning horn is heard which increases in intensity until the actual height is reached when it stops.

Briefing. The Captain gives a comprehensive briefing on the approach and landing he is going to carry out.

He calculates — and this calculation is confirmed by the Co-pilot and Flight Engineer — the distance from MARTIN to begin deceleration. A table takes into consideration the height just before deceleration, the supersonic wind velocity because he expects to be cleared to FL37.0 (37,000ft) and he will become subsonic at FL41.0. In the summer months this distance is in the region of 160nm from MARTIN, but every flight is slightly different and the figure is worked out to the nearest mile. The Captain makes sure that each crew member has the let-down procedure in front of him during the briefing. Each crew member has a booklet — provided in the aircraft library — for London Heathrow, which shows the approach procedure for each runway. The expected runway is 27L and the Captain briefs for a Reduced Noise Approach for this runway, making the ILS frequency the height at the outer marker (OM) which is a radio beacon used to check height on the approach (1,320ft at OM for Runway 27L), and the procedure for a missed approach. The pilot always has to be ready to climb the aircraft back into the air if anything unusual happens during the approach. The most common reasons are aircraft ahead not vacating the runway soon enough, or the pilot not making visual contact at Decision Altitude due to sudden deterioration in the visibility or cloud base.

A Reduced Noise Approach is, as its name implies, a procedure which keeps the engine noise of the aircraft as low as possible for the people living on the approach path. The aircraft is flown at 190kt until 800ft when the automatic throttle, which has already been primed to the target threshold speed of

153kt+7kt=160kt, is adjusted to bring the speed down from 190kt to 160kt. The speed stabilises at 160kt at 500ft. This means that the aircraft has descended at reduced power — and therefore reduced noise — from 800ft to 500ft on the approach and also, prior to that, has been flying at 190kt — which is 30kt above final approach speed — using a lower pitch attitude and therefore less engine power, producing less noise on the ground.

Co-pilot: 'London, Speedbird 2 request decel and descent clearance.'
LATCC: 'Speedbird 2 you are cleared to Flight Level 37.0 after passing 8° West.'

There are crossing airways underneath which produce this restriction. The cleared altitude is noted in the log but is not yet set in the Altitude Select window, 41,000ft is selected at first. The reason for this will become apparent later. The crew are very carefully watching the miles to MARTIN ticking off on the No 3 INS which previously has been set 0-1 (from present position to MARTIN), and at 170 miles to go the Flight Engineer begins to pump fuel forward from the 57.5% C of G position, which he achieved towards the end of the cruise procedure, towards 55% which is the subsonic position again. He has previously calculated the amount of fuel to be pumped forward.

At 160 miles to go, the Captain calls for the first reduction of power to 18deg of throttle angle. This power is nowhere near idle thrust because a considerable amount of power is required to keep a good flow of air through the cabin air control system.

The Captain selects ALT HOLD on the AFCS (Automatic Flight Control System) panel and as power is reduced the Mach number begins to reduce at a constant altitude.

Speed is carefully monitored until the indicated airspeed (IAS) reaches 360kt and the Altitude Acquire button is pressed — remember, 41,000ft has been set in this window — and the aircraft automatically begins descending at 800ft/min. When the speed reaches 350kt the IAS Hold button is pressed. This will maintain 350kt and therefore the descent rate will increase rapidly. All the way down a very careful watch is kept on the relationship between Mach number and the distance to MARTIN. It is very convenient that the digits after the decimal point of the Mach meter should equal the distance to go after Mach 1.5 (ie, Mach 1.*50* should mean that there are *50* miles to go to the Mach 1 point). The calculated distance is obviously only correct if

the parameters used are similar to the actual conditions during the descent.

At Mach 1.5 a further power reduction to 32° of throttle angle is possible because the reduced mass flow in the cabin is acceptable. The aircraft therefore descends even more quickly. If the Captain decides that Mach 1 is not going to be achieved by 55 miles to MARTIN, he can further reduce the power consistent with adequate mass flow in the cabin or, if he is very fast, he may press MACH HOLD at Mach 1.3 and the aircraft will descend very rapidly to 41,000ft and fly level for a while with idle power, thus allowing the Mach number to reduce rapidly in the last stages of the deceleration procedure in level flight. If the aircraft has decelerated more quickly than the calculation suggested, then an early arrival at Mach 1 is accepted as no boom problem will occur.

The reason for not selecting 37,000ft in the Altitude Select window at the beginning is an engine consideration. The engines have been at low power during the descent and if the aircraft was flown straight down to 37,000ft, a large power increment would be required to maintain cruise subsonic Mach number of 0.95. This means the engine temperatures would increase rapidly with possible uneven heating taking place. To prolong engine life it is necessary to set a fixed power of 86% for 1min so the aircraft is levelled at 41,000ft and when the speed is below Mach 1, power is increased by the Flight Engineer to 86% and is carefully monitored for 1min. In the meantime 37,000ft is set in the window and Mach 0.95 is maintained on the AFCS. After 1min the automatic throttles are engaged again and the normal subsonic cruise is maintained when the aircraft reaches 37,000ft.

The deceleration is obviously one of the more critical parts of the flight and very careful monitoring by all crew members is required and, of course, the Captain has kept the passengers informed on the PA of the deceleration and descent details. The cabin is now being prepared for the landing and all those who are interested have visited the flightdeck to have their Concorde Certificates signed by the Captain. Occasionally, someone very interested in flying is allowed to sit in the fourth (jump) seat for the landing.

Concorde now behaves like any subsonic airliner again and has to fit in with the normal airways traffic pattern for the approach to Heathrow. The Flight Engineer has obtained the arrival information from London ATC:

LATCC: 'This is Heathrow Information

"Quebec" at 17.15 hours — 240/20 10K — 4 oktas 5,000ft — temperature 15, dewpoint 4, ONH 1013, landing Runway 27L. Advise aircraft type and information Quebec received on first contact with Heathrow Approach.'

This weather causes no problem as the wind is from 240° (SW) at 20kt, the visibility is 10km, the cloud is half cover (4/8) at 5,000ft and the temperature is, as forecast, 15°C or 59°F. The Captain confirms his briefing still applies and has a final word with the passengers after ascertaining that there will be a 10min delay before he is allowed to land. This is a little annoying to both passengers — who may have tight onward connections — and the crew who know that Concorde sells speed, and to have to hold not only upsets the passengers but uses more fuel, especially at slow speeds.

However, a condition of Concorde being allowed to operate into and out of Heathrow was that it should be treated in the same way as any other aircraft and should be given no special priority. Air Traffic Controllers on both sides of the Atlantic are extremely helpful and Concorde crews are always very appreciative, doing all they can to comply with instructions. But Concorde is a different aircraft and this has to be understood by crews and controllers alike in order to allow the aircraft to operate efficiently.

One of these differences is the speed Concorde can maintain in a holding pattern. London ATC has ordered Concorde 2 to proceed direct to OCKHAM, the holding area south of Heathrow, and hold. The delay will be approximately 10min. When Concorde slows down in level flight the first noticeable phenomenon is the increase in power required to maintain level flight at 250kt because the attitude of the aircraft increases and the aerodynamic drag increases as the vast delta wing is presented to the airflow as a large air brake, requiring high power to keep her level. The fuel flow is at least 13,000kg/hr so 10min will burn in excess of 2,100kg. This is acceptable today because the Captain loaded an extra 3,000kg of fuel for just this situation, but any longer delay would have eaten into fuel reserves and a diversion to Gatwick may have resulted. There have been very few Concorde diversions from Heathrow because the arrival schedules are, except for one, outside the usual 'rush hour' at the airport.

On this occasion the arrival time at Heathrow should be 18.10 GMT (19.10 BST).

Approaching London, Concorde is transferred to London Control on 133.6 and given a descent clearance to descend to FL80 to cross abeam KENNET at FL110 or below, and continue direct to OCKHAM. The Co-pilot acknowledges this clearance and the Captain re-primes the AFCS to descend the aircraft in 'vertical-speed' mode at a descent rate of 2,500ft/min and the automatic throttles are keeping the speed at 350kt indicated. The INS is steering Concorde direct to OCKHAM.

The Captain calls for the Approach Check List and the Flight Engineer begins the fairly long check.

Flight Engineer: 'Landing Briefing.'

Left:
Both speed and altitude wind down as Concorde is prepared for the final stages of the flight.

Above:
Nose is at 5° with the visor down and airspeed at 250kt during the intermediate approach. Autopilot is still engaged.

The Captain responds that there is no change to the Landing Briefing for Runway 27L. The taxi/turn lights are switched on. These lights are illuminated in terminal areas to help other pilots to see any aircraft close to them. The cabin signs are switched on indicating that the passengers must return to their seats and fasten their seat belts ready for landing; the stewardess announces this instruction on the PA. Engine controls are set for landing and the fuel system, electrical system and centre of gravity are all prepared for landing; the crew seats and harnesses are secure and locked. The aircraft is now ready — apart from the Landing Check — for landing.

At OCKHAM at 8,000ft, with the autopilot still engaged and the speed at 250kt, the Captain adjusts the heading to fly outbound in the racetrack holding pattern for 1min. Concorde holds a little faster than other aircraft to reduce the pitch attitude — and therefore the engine power required — to maintain level flight, keeping fuel consumption to an acceptable level for a short while.

The aircraft is turned back towards OCKHAM; it must not pass more than nine miles south of OCKHAM or it will interfere with Gatwick traffic.

Heathrow Approach: 'Speedbird 2, this is Heathrow Approach, you are cleared to FL70 and next time over OCKHAM turn on to a heading of 070°'.
Co-pilot: 'Speedbird 2 is cleared to FL70 and heading 070 at OCKHAM.'

The crew are pleased that the delay has turned out to be less than 10min and they are now cleared for the intermediate approach into Heathrow, and can hear the other aircraft ahead being cleared to lower altitudes and being told to change frequency. Another aircraft, an Air France Airbus, passes below them climbing out towards the south coast of England, on its way to Paris.

The Captain watches the OCKHAM VOR needle flick round from pointing forward to pointing to the rear, meaning he has passed over OCKHAM and he is now able to turn the heading knob to read 070°. The aircraft begins

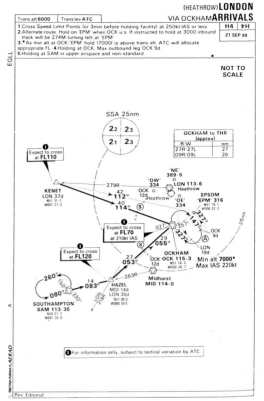

Above:
'Speedbird 2, this is Heathrow Approach. You are cleared to FL7.0 and next turn over OCKHAM turn on to a heading of 070°.' *Jonathan Falconer*

Above right:
London Heathrow Standard Arrivals Chart.
Courtesy British Airways AERAD

to turn from heading 327° towards 070° and the altimeter shows approaching FL70. The ALT ACQ light illuminates, meaning the auto-pilot is about to level the aircraft at FL70.

Heathrow Approach: 'Speedbird 2, change to Heathrow Director on 120.4.'
Co-pilot: 'Heathrow Director, this is Speedbird Concorde 2 FL70.'
Heathrow Approach: 'Speedbird Concorde 2, descend to 3,000ft on QNH 1013.'
Co-pilot: 'Speedbird 2 is cleared to 3,000ft on 1013.'

The Captain selects 3,000ft in ALT SELECT and presses ALT ACQ under which a triangular light appears to show that the new altitude is primed.

Captain: '3,000 checked.'

Both other crew members check the correct cleared altitude is set in the window.

Heathrow Approach: 'Speedbird 2 is No 5 to land with 18 miles to go.'
Co-pilot: 'Roger, Speedbird 2.'

The INS is set 0-5 which means present position to way-point 5, which is the position of the Terminal Building where Concorde will park. This gives the crew another indication of how far the aircraft has to fly to Heathrow and it backs up the distance shown on the DME read-out when the ILS is selected on both pilots' receivers.

Concorde 2 is now heading in the opposite direction to the runway heading, descending and waiting its turn to commence final approach.

On the Captain's side of the flightdeck, the ILS frequency 109.5MHz is selected and the runway heading 275°M is set in the VOR/LOC window on the combing; the callsign is checked, the distance to touchdown appears in the DME read-out and is the primary check of distance to go. The Co-pilot keeps his VOR on

Above left:
'The Approach Checklist is complete.' Taxi/turn
lights are switched on.

Left:
Concorde approaches London Heathrow Airport.

Above:
'Established on the ILS at 190kt.'

'LOW' to give a general heading and distance
to the airport to check that the ILS is giving a
correct indication on the Captain's side.

The medium frequency beacons are tuned to
the 'Outer Marker' (OM) 334kHz, and the
callsign 'OE' checked on both. The projected
height of the aircraft at the Outer Marker is
confirmed by the Co-pilot.

Heathrow Approach: 'Speedbird Concorde 2,
turn left on to 360° base leg and reduce speed
to 190kt and maintain till the Outer Marker.'
Co-pilot: 'Speedbird 2, left on to 360° and
speed 190kt.'

This speed restriction fits in well with the
approach phase because the speed is already
in the process of being reduced from 250kt to
210kt; 190kt will now be dialled in the IAS ACQ

window so the autothrottles will open up when
the speed gets to 190kt and this will be
maintained until a further selection is made.
The ILS provides guidance in two planes: the
Localiser in the horizontal plane and, if the
Localiser bar is kept in the centre of the
display, the aircraft is heading correctly along
the extended centreline of the runway — in
this case 275°M. The Glideslope takes care of
the vertical plane and if correctly flown will
allow the aircraft to descend, by keeping the
bar in the middle, on a 3° Glideslope to the
correct touchdown point on the runway.

The Captain is about to carry out a Reduced
Noise Approach followed by a manual landing
so he presses the autopilot disconnect button
on the control column: there is a warning
'bleep' as the autopilot disconnects and the
Captain levels the aircraft at 3,000ft, 190kt and
a heading of 360°. The attitude of the aircraft
in this configuration is 10° nose-up.

Distance from touchdown is now 13 miles
and the aircraft is approaching the Localiser.
Both pilots had been able to see Heathrow
when they were descending below 5,000ft and
they now have a good view of the runway over
to the left, just before they turn on to final
approach. They can also see two aircraft
further down and another about six miles
ahead of them so they can see they are well
positioned in the queue for landing.

Heathrow Approach: 'Speedbird 2, turn left
on to 310 and intercept the Localiser for
Runway 27L. Call established and descend to
2,500ft.'
Co-pilot: 'Concorde 2 is cleared to heading
310° and will call established.'

In the ALT ACQ window 2,500ft is set and
descent is commenced.

Co-pilot: 'Localiser active.'

The yellow bar begins to move across each of
the two main instruments — ADI (Attitude
Director Indicator) and the HSI (Horizontal
Situation Indicator). Simultaneously the Captain turns the aircraft to the left towards a
heading of 275° and, as the aircraft intercepts
the correct Localiser heading, the VOR/LOC
light illuminates confirming Localiser capture.

Co-pilot: 'VOR/LOC capture.'

The Flight Engineer has, by now, turned his
seat to face forward and is as far forward as he
can be. Busily monitoring engine instruments

Left:
Concorde in the landing configuration: attitude 11°, airspeed 160kt.

Above:
Runway ahead:
Co-pilot **'Speedbird 2, established Runway 27L.'**

he is also a third very valuable pair of eyes monitoring the flying of the aircraft, altimeter readings, autothrottle selections and radio aids. He has the check list ready to read the Landing Check.

Co-pilot: 'Glideslope active.'

The Glideslope bar leaves its position at the top of the two instruments and when it is two dots from the centre, the Captain calls for the gear down and Landing Check List.

Flight Engineer: 'Landing Check List.'

The Co-pilot selects the gear lever 'DOWN'.

Flight Engineer: 'Landing gear.'
Captain and Co-pilot: 'Four greens.'

This means that the green lights denoting all four wheels locked down are illuminated: nosewheel, mainwheels and tailwheel.

The Flight Engineer presses the Cabin Crew Call button on the roof panel three times. This tells the cabin crew in the cabin that the aircraft is about to land and they must get to their landing positions and strap themselves in.

Flight Engineer: 'Nose.'

The Co-pilot selects the nose to its lowest position of 12.5° down, and another green light illuminates.

Co-pilot: 'Down and green.'
Flight Engineer: 'Brakes.'

The Co-pilot checks the eight antiskid lights on his lower front panel and then makes sure the brake lever is in the normal position and presses the brake pedals.

Co-pilot: 'Checked.'

The Flight Engineer completes the landing check silently, checking the radar off and the

'yellow' hydraulic system checked and ready to be used if there is a failure of either of the other two systems — blue or green. He then puts his check list down to concentrate on monitoring the landing. He is in a slightly awkward position in that he cannot see out of the aircraft at all during the approach because of the high nose-up attitude, so he can only carefully watch the instruments.

The Captain has noted that the aircraft is now on the Glideslope so he follows his Flight Director which guides him down the Glideslope. He flies the aircraft with his left hand and rests his right hand on the throttles, feeling their movement as they keep the airspeed within one or two kt of 190. Because the pilots are right at the front of the fuselage and their seats are elevated, they have a very good view from the aircraft in spite of the nose-up attitude. No part of the structure in front of the windscreen is visible.

Co-pilot: 'Speedbird 2, established Runway 27L.'
Heathrow Approach: 'Speedbird 2, call Heathrow Tower on 118.5MHz and report the Outer Marker.'

Above:
***Heathrow Tower* 'Speedbird 2 is cleared to land Runway 27L, wind 260/15.'** *Jonathan Falconer*

Co-pilot: 'Heathrow Tower, Speedbird 2 is at the Outer Marker.'
Heathrow Tower: 'Speedbird 2 continue, one touching down.'
Co-pilot: 'Speedbird 2 continue.'

The Captain makes very slight movements on the control column now because the wind is not strong; the approach is fairly smooth with occasional turbulence as the ground gets closer.

Heathrow Tower: 'Speedbird 2 is cleared to land Runway 27L, wind 260/15.'
Co-pilot: 'Speedbird 2, cleared to land.'
Flight Engineer: '1,000ft Radio.'
Co-pilot: 'Go around height set, five greens.'

He has checked the four undercarriage lights and one visor/nose light; he has set 3,000ft in the ALT SELECT window in case a landing is not possible and a climb to 3,000ft is required.

Flight Engineer: '800ft.'

The Captain responds to that call from the Flight Engineer by pressing his IAS ACQ button which has been previously selected to the reference speed of 160kt (VREF+7), and the throttles close a little. The speed begins to reduce from 190kt towards 160. The Captain raises the nose slightly, easing back on the control column, still following the Glideslope, but flying at an increased attitude (10.5°) to maintain 160kt. At the '500ft' call by the

Flight Engineer: '500ft.'
Co-pilot: 'Speed stabilised at 160kt.'

Flight Engineer: '400ft.'

Co-pilot: '100 above.'

This means 100ft above the decision height for this approach — 300ft. The Captain must not descend lower without having the runway in sight.

Flight Engineer: '300ft.'
Co-pilot: 'Decide.'

Captain: 'Land.'

The Captain then calls for the Flight Directors to be switched off and he concentrates on maintaining an attitude of 10.5° and speed of 160kt.
At 300ft the beginning of 'Ground Effect' is felt. Ground Effect is the cushioning of air between those big delta wings and the ground and it manifests itself on Concorde at about 300ft causing a slight rumbling noise which can be heard by the crew. The Captain maintains the Glideslope until 200ft and then stabilises the attitude of the aircraft at 10.75°.

Flight Engineer: '200ft, 100ft, 50, 40 . . .'

At 40ft the Captain disconnects the auto-throttles by pressing the button on the throttles with his thumb.

Flight Engineer: '30, 20, 15ft.'

At 20ft a very slight back-pressure on the control column is necessary and at 15ft the Captain slowly closes the throttles. As he does so the aircraft tends to pitch down so he eases back on the column, keeping the attitude of 10.75°. The aircraft should settle gently on the mainwheels.
Immediately, the throttles are selected to 'Reverse Idle' which closes the 'clam' doors at

Left:
Flight Engineer
'30 . . . 20 . . . 15ft . . .'

55

the back of each engine, pushing air forwards.

The nose, which seems very high on landing, is allowed to drop gently until the nosewheel contacts the ground. The brakes are then applied and the throttles pulled back into 'Engine Reverse.'

Reverse engine power is very effective at the higher speeds during the landing roll, but at 100kt, the outboard engines are pushed to 'Reverse Idle.' At 75kt the inboard throttles join the others at 'Reverse Idle' and by 40kt all engines are returned to 'Forward Thrust' and the aircraft brakes bring Concorde to a halt about two-thirds of the way down the runway.

The aircraft will stop very quickly if full braking is used, but this causes unnecessary wear and is used only on short runways.

Captain: 'After Landing Check List, please.'
Concorde 2 turns left on to the taxiway. The Co-pilot puts the nose back to 5° for taxying and switches off the main landing lights, leaving the two turn-off lights.

Heathrow Tower: 'Speedbird 2 landed at 03, clear left and call Ground on 121.9.' This is the final call from Heathrow Tower and the Co-pilot changes to the Heathrow Ground frequency.

Co-pilot: 'Speedbird 2 is clear of 27L.'

Heathrow Ground: 'Speedbird 2 follow the greens to Tango 7.' Tango 7 is the gate in Terminal 4 to which Concorde will taxi and by which it will park to allow the jetty to be manoeuvred up against the front left-hand door to facilitate the disembarkation of the passengers.

As Concorde comes to a halt on Gate T7, correctly positioned by the Captain obeying a number of lights to guide him to the correct stopping place on the correct centreline, the Co-pilot selects nose-up and then the visor-up and the Captain selects the brakes to 'Park.'

As they depart Concorde, the passengers are usually very appreciative of the hard-working cabin crew and they nearly all murmur their thanks as they pass the Cabin Service Director at the door. Many of them will be travelling on Concorde again soon, back to America, their business complete.

At landing weight, Concorde can be taxied easily on two engines so the Flight Engineer stops the inboard engines (Nos 2 and 3) for the taxi to the gate and on arrival he shuts down the remaining left-hand engine (No 1). No 4 is left running to maintain electrical power until ground power is plugged into the socket by the nosewheel.

Ground Engineer: 'Chocks in, ground power connected.'

Below:
Shimmering in its own jet efflux, Concorde taxies towards the Terminal.

Above and below left:
Taxying in at Heathrow: 'Speedbird 2, follow the greens to Tango 7', comes the call from Heathrow Ground Control.

The Flight Engineer acknowledges and notes that the 'Ground Power' light is illuminated and he switches to 'Ground Power' and then closes the high pressure fuel cock of the final engine.

The Shutdown Check is carried out by the flightdeck crew. The Co-pilot checks and records the error in the INS and finds that No 1 is one mile out in 3,147nm; No 2 is one mile out, but No 3 is four miles out. This last error is still within the laid-down tolerances of the system.

Running through his check list, the Flight Engineer switches off all systems and records the amount of fuel remaining in the Technical Log. On this occasion, remembering that there was a short delay at OCKHAM, the fuel remaining was 10,900kg; 9,200kg is the calculated reserve fuel, for a diversion to Gatwick — 2,700 for the journey and 6,500 as reserve fuel. So the fuel flight plan on this occasion was very accurate.

The Flight Engineer now records any defects occurring on the flight in the Technical Log. On this trip he noted that a 'lane' had failed in the engine intake system: operation had been on

Above:
The Captain prepares to disembark at Heathrow's Terminal 4 after running through the Shutdown Checklist.

Below:
London Heathrow Aerodrome Taxi Chart.
Courtesy British Airways AERAD

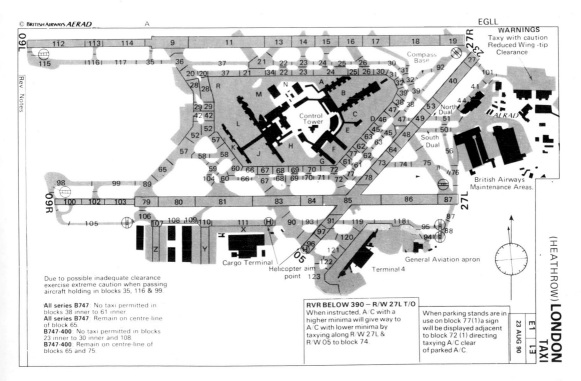

© BRITISH AIRWAYS *AERAD*

EGLL

WARNINGS
Taxy with caution
Reduced Wing-tip
Clearance

Compass Base

Control Tower

North Dual

South Dual

British Airways Maintenance Areas.

Cargo Terminal

Helicopter aim point

Terminal 4

General Aviation apron

Due to possible inadequate clearance exercise extreme caution when passing aircraft holding in blocks 35, 116 & 99.

All series B747: No taxi permitted in blocks 38 inner to 61 inner
All series B747: Remain on centre-line of block 65.
B747-400: No taxi permitted in blocks 23 inner to 30 inner and 108.
B747-400: Remain on centre-line of blocks 65 and 75.

RVR BELOW 390 — R/W 27L T/O
When instructed, A/C with a higher minima will give way to A/C with lower minima by taxying along R/W 27L & R/W 05 to block 74.

When parking stands are in use on block 77(1)a sign will be displayed adjacent to block 72 (1) directing taxying A/C clear of parked A/C.

23 AUG 90   E1 L3

(HEATHROW) LONDON TAXI

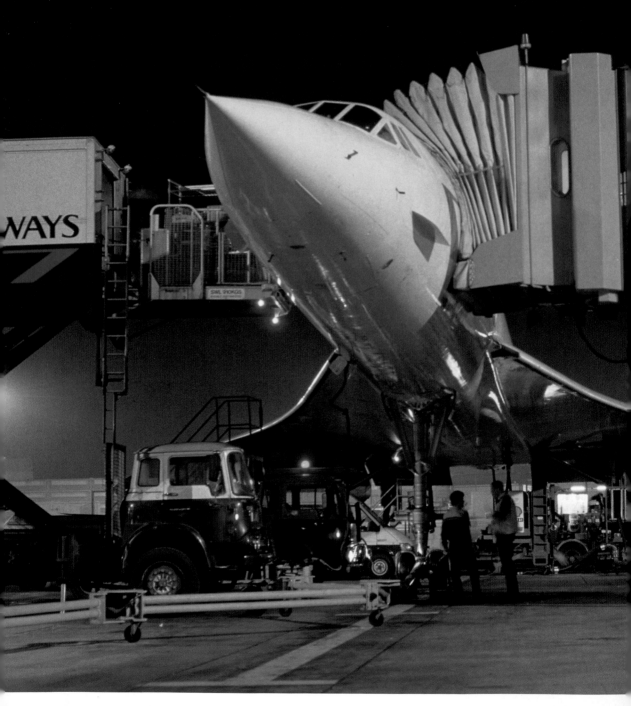

Nocturne in gold: on the ramp at Terminal 4, mission accomplished.

the other electrical signalling lane. One brake had failed, the forward left-hand wheel was cold when the others were all approximately 200°C. Finally he records the radiation meter reading. Concorde is the only airliner equipped with a radiation meter. All readings are recorded and sent to the British Airline Pilots' Association Technical Committee which keeps an eye on the doses of radiation experienced by the crew to make sure that their members are protected. British Airways doctors analyse the readings and find that Concorde crews receive little more radiation in Concorde than other crews did when special comparisons were carried out 10 years ago.

Passengers have disembarked, the cabin crew have said goodbye — most of them are working the next day on a Boeing 737 or 757 on the short-haul routes, and then another Concorde trip a couple of days later. The Captain, Co-pilot and Flight Engineer talk to the Ground Engineers about the snags on the aircraft — not many today — and discuss when 'AB' will be flying again. It is scheduled to operate Speedbird 001 tomorrow at 10.30am to JFK.

G-BOAC

Left:
The maintenance effort required to keep British Airways' fleet of seven Concordes flying is both large and impressive: some 56 man-hours of maintenance at the airline's Heathrow Engineering Base are required to keep Concorde in the air for just one hour.

Below left:
Concorde 'AB' is pictured in British Airways' Technical Block B where she is about to have one of her Rolls-Royce SNECMA Olympus 593 turbojets replaced. Access to the engines for regular inspection is gained through large downward-opening doors in the undersides of the nacelles.

Right:
A Major Maintenance Check is undertaken every 12,000hr and takes approximately three months to complete. All Concorde's external paint is stripped down to the bare metal, internal fittings are removed, the four engines are taken out together with their intakes, access panels and doors are also removed. Electrical cable runs are replaced because they become worn owing to high frequency vibration during supersonic flight. Concorde 'AD' is pictured halfway through her 'Major' at Heathrow on 11 January 1989. *Jonathan Falconer*

Routine maintenance complete, Concorde is ready to be towed to Terminal 4 in preparation for an evening departure to New York.

The crew can look back on this sector as a very normal operation, but there is no chance of being bored: Concorde is an exciting aircraft to fly because it keeps everyone on their toes. It always wants to go faster and, indeed, is happier faster. When climbing in the early stages of flight there is a continuous slight buffet of the outer elevons when the attitude is 7.5° and above. This disappears to absolutely smooth flight as the attitude is reduced and speed increased. When approaching VMO (maximum operating speed) in the climb the pilot has to be careful not to exceed this speed (400kt) at 5,000ft and above, as the speed needle rapidly approaches the yellow VMO needle, especially when the aircraft is light. Sometimes, on the short charters round the Scilly Isles out of Heathrow when the take-off weight is only 125 tonnes and the acceleration down the runway is phenomenal, it is quite difficult to level the aircraft at 3,000ft when required, even though the Noise Abatement cutback is used. These short charters, which cost around £450 for a flight of 1hr 40min from terminal to terminal, allow a large cross-section of the public to experience the Concorde flight regime and fly supersonically even for a short while. The route is the normal one which takes Concorde over Reading and Bristol, first flying at 28,000ft at Mach 0.95 and then accelerating and climbing once over the Bristol Channel.

As the weight is low the acceleration is quick and Mach 2 and 50,000ft is reached in a few minutes. At 06° 45'W a left turn is made, keeping a constant distance from a centre-of-turn point and checking distances from Land's End, as a heading towards Guernsey is achieved and deceleration is started to avoid booming Guernsey. Usually 52,000ft is reached before deceleration. The Flight Engineer is exceedingly busy on this short trip because he still has to pump fuel aft to match C of G with centre of lift movement, and almost immediately forward again as Concorde slows down.

Passengers on this short sector expect to be allowed to see the flightdeck. An extra Pilot or Flight Engineer is carried purely to explain — on the PA — the operation, give a potted history of the aircraft and show passengers the flightdeck for a couple of minutes to allow them to take photographs. This crew member keeps the actual operating crew away from passengers' questions, thus making the whole operation safer. Many destinations are used for charter flights contracted by all types of organisations. Goodwood Travel Ltd of Canterbury charters Concorde almost every week and sometimes more for destinations varying from New York, Moscow, Cairo and Nice, to a complete round-the-world air cruise when 98 passengers fly round the world supersonically whenever possible, stopping at eight different places for a day or two. This is a really luxurious and interesting flight taken by a cross-section of British, European and American passengers. They pay a large amount of money for these charters and yet the flights are oversubscribed.

These trips are a breath of fresh air to crews who seldom get the chance to fly outside the Atlantic environment, but things are changing slowly. The aircraft is becoming popular in the West Indies — Barbados in particular.

So far, a trip from New York to London and the short charters have been described in detail. Concorde is used for many purposes from a private charter where one person

collects together 99 of his friends and wants to fly to some exotic European destination for lunch and a sightseeing tour and return on the same day, to a firm which uses the aircraft as an incentive tool to take employees away for the day or just into the air supersonically for two hours over the Bay of Biscay, having a luxury champagne lunch and returning to Heathrow.

These flights require meticulous planning because the customer, who is paying a considerable fee to charter Concorde, obviously requires the best of everything. With Air Traffic Control difficulties especially during the summer, even Concorde gets delayed by 'slot' difficulties and this is extremely frustrating for passengers and crew who can do nothing to ease this situation. At least Concorde passengers can be accommodated in a separate lounge and served with drinks and snacks, but nevertheless people become very angry. This is where a good Captain, Pilot or Flight Engineer PR man comes into his own, because he will go along to the passenger lounge and explain all the difficulties to the passengers and the charterer. When information comes from the 'horse's mouth' it is easier to understand and sound more genuine than an impersonal announcement over the departure lounge PA system.

Below:
Up above the world so high: a dramatic view of the reheats just after take-off from Heathrow as Concorde 'AA' heads out on a short night charter to the Scilly Isles. *K. Pettit via David Leney*

The fires are lit: another supersonic journey begins.

During 1988 and 1989 five Concordes were undergoing their 12,000hr Major Check. This is the biggest maintenance overhaul in the life of the aircraft and it takes upwards of three months. It is interesting to note that it has taken Concorde 12 years to achieve this number of hours and shows that, although the aircraft has been flying for that time, only 1,000hr/yr has been achieved. A Boeing 747 would fly 4,000hr/yr.

You may wonder why Concorde flies so little: it is a difficult aircraft to schedule across the Atlantic because it is very fast and because there are night jet bans in America and Europe. One Concorde leaves London at 10.30am local time, arriving in New York at 9.20am (New York time). This same aircraft leaves JFK at 13.45pm arriving in London at 10.25pm just in time to beat the London night jet ban (11.00pm).

Another aircraft leaves London at 7.00pm and arrives at JFK at 5.55pm. A quick turnround would be desirable but the London night jet ban has already started.

British Airways thought of scheduling a Concorde to fly from New York at 9.45pm, but it would arrive in London at 6.25am — ie, before the London night jet ban had finished. If it was delayed at all out of New York the JFK night jet ban would ground it at 10.00pm. So you can see that it is very difficult to schedule three Atlantic services each way per day at times when they are commercially acceptable. The other reason that Concorde has not flown many hours per year is that British Airways wants to keep Concorde flying for as long as possible and at the present rate of utilisation people will still be able to fly in Concorde at the end of this century.

Although the preceding paragraphs have been a digression from the description of the charter programme, it is necessary in order to get all aspects of the operation in perspective. Whereas the scheduled Concordes usually fly like clockwork across the Atlantic — and this, in itself, is a major achievement — the round-the-world charters require the greatest planning input.

Up to September 1989 Concorde had flown five trips round the world. Each had gone without a hitch except for a delay on the first sector of one, and a rudder problem in Sydney on the last trip which will be described later.

Planning for the charters begins up to two years before departure date. The charter operator chooses the route he will be able to sell more easily. Cities are chosen either for their interesting historical aspects, climate and tourist facilities, and usually a combination of both appears in the itinerary.

British Airways is approached and has to decide whether Concorde is allowed into the airport: for instance, San Francisco and Los Angeles ban supersonic operations, so Oakland is used because it is slightly less noise-sensitive. A representative from British Airways will then visit the airport if Concorde has not operated through there before. If there are noise or operational points to be discussed a pilot must visit — the author in this case. If the airport is one regularly served by British Airways then the airline's local Station Manager can do the job more than adequately.

A contract is produced which is extremely complicated and must take into consideration every aspect of the operation which could go wrong. It must always be remembered that there are 100 passengers who have sometimes paid more than £20,000 each for their trip of a lifetime. and justifiably they expect every contingency to be covered.

The worst worry is a breakdown of the aircraft. A comprehensive spares pack, containing necessary small items and a spare wheel is carried on board, but larger parts must either be positioned at strategic airports along the route or be ferried out from London. As it takes subsonic aircraft currently in service nearly 24hr to get to Sydney, for instance, it is a costly business to position spares at all ports of call. If an engine fails, and Concorde has the same problems as any other aircraft, one must be ferried from London in the hold of a Boeing 747. It is an occurrence which is catered for, but hopefully will not happen, because obviously British Airways will be responsible for any defect on the aircraft.

Up to six months before the day of departure, a big meeting is held in London encompassing all the departments involved in the planning process. The meeting is usually chaired by the Charter Sales Manager and includes the following:

- **The Charterer and his Representatives.** They put all their ideas forward, especially concerning passenger needs during their flights.
- **Security.** One of the most important aspects these days is the security of the aircraft and baggage at all stages. A security guard, sometimes local — and sometimes specially flown from London — looks after passenger baggage from the time the passenger puts it outside his bedroom door until it arrives at the next hotel several

thousand miles away. There is a guard on Concorde 24hr a day wherever she is parked.

- **Catering.** British Airways produces several menu choices on board Concorde and the charterers and British Airways decide together on the best menu. Some passengers prefer local food, some European or American; most prefer small quantities and all want quite a lot to drink ranging from soft drinks to champagne to spirits. Obviously only a certain amount can be carried in Concorde's limited galley area so a very careful choice must be made. If passenger needs are not met, a change during the trip is possible, so that satisfaction is guaranteed on the next sector.

A special British Airways catering expert will personally supervise every meal produced. He will position himself to the next-but-one station to prepare for Concorde's arrival there.

- **Navigation Officer.**
- **Flight Manager Technical** (who is Captain). As you know Concorde can usually only fly supersonically over the water and over some parts of Australia and Egypt so, except for one round-the-world trip which was totally supersonic, there were several subsonic sectors overland.

The whole route is analysed by the Flight Manager Technical (FMT) and his Navigation Superintendent and many overflight clearances have to be granted. Every Air Traffic Control authority must know the operational capabilities of the aircraft and its special needs in case of emergencies. The Navigation Officer produces charts for each sector with the exact track specially drawn.

When Concorde is supersonic there are several technical faults which, if they occur, render the aircraft incapable of remaining supersonic, whereupon she gently descends to subsonic altitudes and speeds. This occurs only occasionally but does cause a marked loss in range and she may be unable to reach her destination subsonically.

A calculation has to be made for each flight showing which alternative airfields can be used on four or three engines, or even two engines, from any point of the track. This is all accomplished very quickly and easily on the Atlantic route but requires a lot of preparation for unusual sectors.

Up until now the Navigation Officer has flown on board the aircraft in order to prepare flight plans at each departure before the crew arrive at the aircraft. Although the crew are perfectly capable themselves of preparing flight plans, the presence of the Navigation

Officer gives added insurance that the aircraft will depart on time with all preliminaries complete. He has proved a saviour on several occasions when communications have broken down between one country and another, both countries or airports not being served normally by British Airways.

- **Cabin Crew Manager.** Two complete crews is the normal complement for a round-the-world charter – one crew operates approximately half the trip, meeting the next crew who have positioned to a suitable halfway city ready to take over. The cabin crew must be briefed on the special needs of each passenger and also make sure that meals specified by the charterer, and agreed by the Catering Manager, are suitable for serving by the cabin crew on that particular sector.

- **Aircrew Facilities Manager.** Hotels for crews must be booked well in advance and it is usually desirable that the crew stay in the same hotel as the passengers so that passengers get to know their crew and vice versa. The crew is sometimes invited to go on tours or attend dinners with the passengers. This is a particularly pleasant part of the trip.

- **Commercial Manager.** He is usually the person involved with the Charter Manager in the signing of the contract and is at the meeting to ensure fair play and make certain that the charterer is not asking for something outside the scope of the contract. He is also highly experienced and able to give advice on all commercial matters.

- **Engineering.** A Maintenance Engineer and a Flight Engineer attend the meeting to decide on the type of engineering cover required at each port of call. Usually a Maintenance Engineer travels with the aircraft throughout the trip. He stays behind after everyone has left the airport to supervise any work which has to be carried out during the stay and make sure Concorde is parked safely and securely. If a major problem occurs he liaises with London during the rectification of the snag and can spend many long hours getting things serviceable for the next departure. The Flight Engineer is not usually required to work on the aircraft on the ground, but is always there in case more help is required.

Sometimes two or three people from a department will attend the meeting as all stations usually require a visit by one person in the department. It is very interesting to see the detailed preparation required for a round-the-world trip, but this is nothing compared with the planning for a Royal Flight.

The last round-the-world trip was planned as totally supersonic, which meant that it was over water all the time and for which the author was Captain for the first half. Three days before departure there was a briefing for the two technical crews involved. Both crews were provided with a large file containing maps, flight plans, communication forms, take-off calculation tables, minimum weather permitted at each airport to be used and everything else required by Pilots and Flight Engineers to complete a safe flight. These files are just for them to peruse before the flight as the aircraft will have all this paperwork in the aircraft's library, carried throughout the trip. The Navigation Officer took both crews through the complete route from the take-off to touchdown on each sector, accentuating the acceleration and deceleration points carefully.

The author briefed on the departure and arrival procedures and parking plans for the Concorde at non-British Airways destinations. Crew allowances were detailed by the Flight Crew Administration Manager, with bill-paying procedures outlined. A Cabin Crew Manager was there to answer any questions and the author confirmed he would be attending the cabin crew briefing the next day.

Accordingly he was introduced to the cabin crew by their manager the next afternoon – he knew most of them because they were experienced Concorde crew members. They also had to volunteer for this particular trip which took them over their normal trip length and as a consequence was treated as a special case by their trade union.

There was a very detailed brief and the author saw every menu and wine choice. Although Concorde always offers excellent wines, the storage facilities on the aircraft are very limited so extra care had to be taken to get things right.

On 31 March 1989 the author and crew left London as passengers. All flights to New York were heavily booked so the technical crew went on Concorde and the cabin crew on the afternoon Boeing 747 flight.

The route in front of them was a very exciting one: New York – Acapulco – Oakland (San Francisco) – Honolulu – Papeete – Christchurch – Sydney. The other crew took over in Sydney and flew to Perth – Colombo – Mombasa – Capetown – Robertsfield (Monrovia) – London. Supersonic all the way except for a very short sector over Mexico to get to Acapulco.

The aircraft itself came from London on a special charter and then was prepared for an afternoon departure from New York on its first leg to Acapulco with a full load of passengers, most of whom were on the trip of a lifetime around the world, but some were guests of the charterer and would be getting off in Oakland. The day was 1 April, a slightly inauspicious day to begin a very important and prestigious trip.

The author's crew consisted of a Co-pilot, Flight Engineer as usual and an extra Captain who was on board to talk to the passengers, tell them about Concorde, the route, and show them the flightdeck when they asked to visit it. The cabin crew consisted of a Cabin Service Director — a very experienced man — and five Stewardesses, all of whom had worked on Concorde for a long time, but all provided the vivacity and charm required by passengers who were used to the very best.

It was important to depart on schedule — as it always is — but this day was something very special. Eventually all the equipment was cleared from around Concorde and they started two engines and pushed back. The taxying time was very short — 5min — and they were soon airborne and away quickly because the aircraft was lighter than normal, requiring less fuel to fly to Acapulco than they used from London (JFK to Acapulco time was 2hr 50min). Acceleration to supersonic speed came soon, just 23min after take-off, and the trip of a lifetime got underway.

The most unusual aspect from an operational point of view was the fact that the route took them between Bimini and the mainland near Miami, a gap of 40 miles, exactly the distance required to prevent a sonic boom on either side. They made sure the navigation computers were fully updated and the view of the whole of Florida and the island of Bimini as they approached the gap was magnificent from 55,000ft. The Florida Keys stretching below were beautiful and soon it was time to decelerate to cross Mexico subsonic, 2hr and 2min after take-off.

In Acapulco the welcome was spectacular, with large crowds and a band to play the passengers down the steps. The British Airways Customer Service Representative was on hand to brief the crew, first on accommodation and allowances and then to discuss the departure for two days hence, with fuel figures and pick-up times agreed. He joined the crew and passengers that evening for a beautiful barbeque at a hotel set in the hillside overlooking the water. With temperatures in the high seventies and the sky clear, the setting was idyllic.

The crew began to become acquainted with their passengers, many of whom had been pilots, and the obvious subject of course was Concorde, her history, her achievements, her performances and her attraction. The enthusiasm for Concorde continues although she has been flying in commercial service since 1976.

On the next day passengers and crew viewed the Acapulco skyline from the sea in a large pleasure cruiser and more friends were made.

The next sector was Acapulco to Oakland where some guests disembarked and the rest of the round-the-world group joined Concorde. Highest altitude reached was 58,000ft and the average speed was 1,024mph.

From Oakland, the departure for Honolulu gives passengers sitting on the right of the aircraft a spectacular view of the city of San Francisco — Concorde was held down at 5,000ft for a few minutes by ATC making it

even more impressive. The aircraft was over water all the way to the Hawaiian Islands and 2hr 20min after take-off Concorde touched down on Runway 08R at Honolulu International Airport. There was no great welcome here because Concorde had been there before and so had most of the passengers. They were departing immediately in a DC-9 to the Island of Mona which offered different facilities from Waikiki, where the crew were staying.

Again all the departure plans were discussed on arrival to ensure that the aircraft was completely ready two days later to meet the returning DC-9. Most of the crew took the wonderful opportunity to visit Pearl Harbor — a very impressive and tasteful monument to that dark day in December 1941 when the Japanese attack brought the USA into World War 2.

The morning of 5 April dawned clear and warm, a distinct difference from the torrential rain and flooding in Oahu the afternoon before, and the crew were sitting waiting for their

Below:
A brief stop was made at Oakland, California, to pick up more passengers.

Left:
Concorde 'AF' heads south between Honolulu and Papeete — just past the equator — as can be seen on the Inertial Navigation System display.

Below:
Arrival in Papeete: the first landing of a British Airways Concorde in Tahiti.

Below right:
With vague echoes of the Rodgers and Hammerstein musical *South Pacific*, the semi-complete transpacific crew are pictured on arrival in Papeete (the photograph was taken by the Co-pilot).

passengers' arrival from Mona. It turned out that no rain had fallen there and our customers had enjoyed a very relaxing two days. It was interesting and very gratifying to note that many of them remarked that they now felt Concorde was their home and they were glad to be back.

Papeete, in the Tahitian Islands, was a place very few people had previously visited so there was an even greater air of excitement as Concorde let down over the water between two islands, having once more achieved 58,000ft and an average speed this time of 1,105mph. The equator was crossed at 55,000ft and many passengers remembered the celebrations at sea when the line is crossed. There was little time for more than a quick sip of champagne as the Captain announced the crossing time. After a flight time of 2hr 31min a smooth touchdown was achieved at the exotic airport at Papeete, and a quick trip to the hotels followed — passengers to one (the most prestigious) and crew to one on the other side

of the island where the sand was volcanic black, which the author found extremely difficult to get used to. The hotel was built into the rock and the crew went down to their rooms from reception — another difficult thing to reckon with especially after a magnificent dinner from the local menu!

Technically, one of the most impressive aspects of the whole tour was the yacht in which they were all taken for a superb cruise the next day. All the sails were computer-controlled and the flightdeck, or perhaps we should say bridge, was composed entirely of video screens and keyboards. The wind speed and directions and desired heading were selected and the sails unfurled, arranging themselves in the most efficient position for those conditions — all by computer. Lunch was taken in paradisaical surroundings on one of the islands.

On 9 April, Concorde taxied down the length of the runway to turn at the end in 150ft, always a manoeuvre to execute carefully, and

Below:
The most distinctive nose in aviation! Concorde is unlikely to be mistaken for any other airliner.

Above:
Lunch was taken in beautiful surroundings on one of the islands. The T-shirts were especially created by the Flight Engineer and the legend reads: 'Trans Pacific Crew: Concorde World Tour '89'.

took-off for Christchurch, New Zealand. It was the first occasion a Concorde had landed at Christchurch and crowds were expected, but not to the extent of the gathering that afternoon. Because there were people gathered on all the roads into the airport the author elected to fly a wide radar/visual circuit of the airport before positioning to land. All roads were blocked and all available vantage points packed to capacity. He found the approach and landing very emotional as he always had done when landing in front of large crowds. A smooth touchdown had to be the order of the day and they taxied in underneath the fine flying display given by a Pitts Special. The passengers disembarked and, after a brief tour of Christchurch and a cocktail reception, were taken to Queenstown, in the heart of South Island.

The author faced the press and cameras and was asked many interesting questions about Concorde and its future. The enthusiasm was overwhelming and their welcome a typical New Zealand one. The crew were generously given tickets to Queenstown the next day and they also were able to marvel at the beauty of the mountains so close to the lake. They flew in

an Islander round the mountains and down to the coast but the weather was not good enough for them to land at Milford Sound, a beautiful mountain-surrounded resort on the west coast.

In the meantime, Concorde had been visited by hundreds of people queuing at the airport to have a look inside and around her. It was quite wet and windy but even that did not seem to deter the crowds.

Next morning a great departure was made from Christchurch for Sydney. The weather was fine but thunderstorms were forecast at Sydney and there was a nagging worry that Air Traffic Controllers would call a lightning strike just before they arrived. There were contingency plans to go to Brisbane if this happened.

On the climb, just after the reheats had been cancelled and normal climb was resumed at just over Mach 1.7, the author felt a small 'thud', almost as if a bird had struck the fuselage — unlikely at 43,000ft. All the instruments were scanned and nothing more could be seen or felt so they continued to accelerate to Mach 2.00 and climb to 55,000ft.

The flight continued quite normally and they obtained descent clearance from Sydney ATC who seemed happy to control Concorde and they decelerated toward Mach 1.3 when there was a continuous vibration felt over the whole aircraft. It was not too bad on the flightdeck, but obviously worse in the cabin. It continued for 2½min during which time the aircraft

Above:

Above:
More in keeping with the results of a World War 2 fighter attack than an exclusive world tour in peacetime, these were the crew's first views of the missing rudder section on arrival in Sydney.

began to slow down more quickly, reducing power on each engine in turn. No change was detected until the vibration became intermittent and then stopped altogether. All indications and handling characteristics were normal and the crew were perplexed and completely baffled as to the cause. The passengers were obviously worried and the author explained that he thought perhaps a panel had come unlocked and had caused the vibration until it had been pulled away from the aircraft by the airflow. This seemed the only explanation and certainly Concorde was behaving normally as the flightdeck crew prepared for the final approach to Runway 34 at Sydney. There was a helicopter on the right-hand side as they passed 500ft and the Co-pilot completed a normal smooth touchdown on schedule. The next radio message from Sydney Tower surprised them.

Sydney Tower: 'Speedbird Concorde Alpha Fox, you have lost half your tail.'

The author asked them to 'say again' because he did not understand what they meant. They repeated that it appeared half the top rudder section had torn off.

They taxied slowly in because there was an aircraft occupying their position at the terminal and when they had stopped, the passengers disembarked and some looked back at Concorde and saw what had happened. They were obviously worried and said so to the many press representatives waiting for them to arrive. The stories going round the world as soon as they landed were, in some cases, far-fetched, so it was decided to call a press conference so that the author could explain what had happened and give the correct story.

In fact, a piece of the top rudder skin had become detached from the honeycomb section to which it was glued and, over a period of 2½min, the skin had peeled off until it came up against something solid, like the hinge of the Power Flying Control Unit. It had stopped then and all had settled down. The bottom rudder section had easily coped, as it is designed to do in the event of a failure in the top section, and

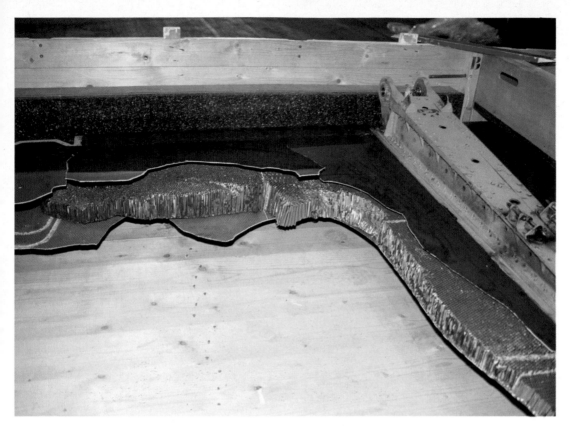

that accounted for the normal handling of Concorde after the incident.

Once it was ascertained by the ground engineers in Sydney what was needed, the British Airways engineers in London sprang into action and in a very short time a new top rudder section was aboard a Boeing 747 bound for Sydney, together with an Air Safety Advisor, two Accident Investigation Officers, a British Aerospace accident expert and two Airframe Engineers.

After a great deal of hard work — day and night — by British Airways and Qantas engineers, the new unit was painted and fitted and Concorde departed Sydney with a completely new crew to begin the second half of her round-the-world cruise only 19hr late.

The author firmly believes that, had it not been for extremely efficient diagnosis and repair and the very quick transportation of the new rudder section, the passengers would have been loathe to board Concorde to continue their journey. As it was, they saw the confidence of the new crew and the author's crew and the author spoke to them all individually during the extra day in Sydney to reassure them. The round-the-world Concorde flight continued to Colombo, via Perth, and regained its schedule. That particular Concorde, G-BOAF, created 15 World Speed Records during the 23 days she was away from London.

For the author, that was a trip to be remembered for all sorts of reasons, least of all the rudder incident. He and his crew finally departed Sydney two days after Concorde, on a Boeing 747, having completed the investigation to the satisfaction of the authorities.

That was to be his last long trip as a Concorde Captain before his retirement in September 1989. He is proud to have been closely associated with the world's first supersonic airliner and he hopes to be able to view the next generation of supersonic transport when it flies — from the flightdeck.